Ethics in a Digital World

Guiding Students Through Society's Biggest Questions

Kristen Mattson

International Society for Technology in Education
PORTLAND, OR ● ARLINGTON, VA

Ethics in a Digital World
Guiding Students Through Society's Biggest Questions
Kristen Mattson

Acquisitions and Developmental Editor: *Valerie Witte*
Copy Editor: *Lisa Hein*
Proofreader: *Linda Laflamme*
Indexer: *Valerie Haynes Perry*
Book Design and Production: *Mayfly Design*
Cover Design: *Beth DeWilde*

Library of Congress Cataloging-in-Publication Data
Names: Mattson, Kristen, author.
Title: Ethics in a digital world : guiding students through society's
   biggest questions / Kristen Mattson.
Description: First edition. | Portland, OR : International Society for
   Technology in Education, [2021] | Includes bibliographical references
   and index.
Identifiers: LCCN 2020056235 (print) | LCCN 2020056236 (ebook) | ISBN
   9781564849014 (paperback) | ISBN 9781564848987 (epub) | ISBN
   9781564848994 (mobi) | ISBN 9781564849007 (pdf)
Subjects: LCSH: Internet—Moral and ethical aspects. | Internet—Social
   aspects. | Internet in education.
Classification: LCC TK5105.878 .M38 2021 (print) | LCC TK5105.878 (ebook) | DDC 175—dc23
LC record available at https://lccn.loc.gov/2020056235
LC ebook record available at https://lccn.loc.gov/2020056236

First Edition
ISBN: 978-1-56484-901-4

Ebook version available

Printed in the United States of America

ISTE® is a registered trademark of the International Society for Technology in Education.

About ISTE

The International Society for Technology in Education (ISTE) is a nonprofit organization that works with the global education community to accelerate the use of technology to solve tough problems and inspire innovation. Our worldwide network believes in the potential technology holds to transform teaching and learning.

ISTE sets a bold vision for education transformation through the ISTE Standards, a framework for students, educators, administrators, coaches and computer science educators to rethink education and create innovative learning environments. ISTE hosts the annual ISTE Conference & Expo, one of the world's most influential edtech events. The organization's professional learning offerings include online courses, professional networks, year-round academies, peer-reviewed journals and other publications. ISTE is also the leading publisher of books focused on technology in education. For more information or to become an ISTE member, visit iste.org. Subscribe to ISTE's YouTube channel and connect with ISTE on Twitter, Facebook and LinkedIn.

Related ISTE Titles

Digital Citizenship in Action: Empowering Students to Engage in Online Communities

By Kristen Mattson

iste.org/DigCitAction

The Digital Citizenship Handbook for School Leaders: Fostering Positive Interactions Online

By Mike Ribble and Marty Park

iste.org/DigCitforLeaders

To see all books available from ISTE, please visit **iste.org/books**

About the Author

 Dr. Kristen Mattson is a wife, mother of three, former English teacher, and school librarian. She is currently an adjunct professor and consultant. She partners with educators in all content areas to integrate digital literacy, research skills, creation, and innovation in the classroom.

Kristen holds a bachelor's degree in education and a master's degree in instructional design and technology, and she earned her doctoral degree in curriculum and instruction leadership from Northern Illinois University in 2016 after conducting a critical discourse analysis on secondary digital citizenship curriculum.

Acknowledgments

I want to thank several individuals who have been instrumental in making this book possible:

- The team at ISTE, including editor Valerie Witte, who saw promise in this work even when I was feeling less than confident about it.

- My graduate students at the University of Illinois who continue to push my thinking even when I am supposed to be pushing theirs.

- My fabulous friends in education, including (but not limited to!) Nancy Watson, LeeAnn Lindsey, and Adam Dyche, who are always willing to ideate with me, read drafts of my work, and offer constructive feedback when I need it.

- My husband, children, and parents. Your unwavering support is the reason I can continue to do what I love. Thank you for that gift.

My biggest debt of gratitude is to the educators featured throughout the book. Thank you for trusting me to write and share your stories. Thank you for the work you do day in and day out as forward-thinking educators, willing to embrace the messy and unpredictable to help students succeed.

Publisher's acknowledgments

ISTE gratefully acknowledges the contributions of the following:

ISTE Standards reviewers

Marcie Hebert
Billy Krakower
Tara Schneider

Manuscript reviewers

Nancy Watson
Vanessa Monterosa

Dedication

For my mom, who claims to be allergic to learning and probably won't read beyond this page. Love you!

Contents

About ISTE iii

About the Author iv

Foreword ix

Introduction 1

What Is in This Book 3

Who This Book Is for 4

Ethics in the Curriculum   5

Frameworks to Situate Digital Ethics Amongst Other Ethical Questions 6

Why Engage Students in Conversations of Tech Ethics? 9

Tips for Successful Discussions 12

Access to Information: Is It Time to Better Regulate the Internet?   19

Building Background Knowledge 20

Breaking Down the Arguments 26

Curricular Connections 35

Privacy in the Digital Age: How Much Are You Willing to Give Up?   41

Building Background Knowledge 42

Breaking Down the Arguments 48

Curricular Connections 60

Human Bias: Can Artificial Intelligence Help Diminish Human Bias in Decision-making?   65

Building Background Knowledge 66

Artificial Intelligence in Decision-making 68

Breaking Down the Arguments 72

Curricular Connections 79

The Future of Work: Is Innovation Helpful or Harmful?   83

Building Background Knowledge 85

Breaking Down the Arguments 88

Curricular Connections 96

Technology and Mental Health: Cause or Cure?   101

Building Background Knowledge 102

Breaking Down the Arguments 108

Curricular Connections 116

Social Media and Society: Flashlight or Flame?   121

Building Background Knowledge 122

Breaking Down the Arguments 126

Curricular Connections 140

Conclusion and Call to Action   143

References 147

Index 157

Foreword

How can we empower students to build a better tech future? It certainly won't happen with a reactive list of digital don'ts.

What has impressed me about the work of Dr. Kristen Mattson is her approach to digital citizenship that focuses on growing thoughtful, empathetic digital citizens who are capable of wrestling with the difficult ethical issues found in our digital world. This stands in direct contrast to so much of the messaging of digital citizenship that treats children and teens as brands that need to be protected, as opposed to humans who need to be developed. As the co-founder of the Digital Citizenship Summit, founded in 2015 to promote "the safe, savvy, and ethical use of social media and technology," I have been drawn to Dr. Mattson's advocacy and scholarship that positions digital citizenship as far more than risk management. It is about making well-rounded students who understand their role in the digital world. As she wrote in *Digital Citizenship in Action: Empowering Students to Engage in Online Communities*, "Digital citizenship curriculum must strive to show students possibilities over problems, opportunities over risks, and community successes over personal gains." I couldn't agree more.

As a frequent speaker and consultant on tech ethics, along with serving on TikTok's Content Advisory Council, I am heartened to see thought leaders like Dr. Mattson push forward the conversation around digital citizenship and ethics in the digital world. Far too often this has been a discussion happening only on college campuses and tech conferences, as opposed to middle schools and high schools. It is crucial that this type of education happens earlier in a student's life, which is why *Ethics in a Digital World* is such a needed book for middle and high school educators.

Similar to her progressive approach to digital citizenship, Dr. Mattson is paving the way for more students to grapple with the complex ethical problems that are plentiful in the digital world. The minefield of issues that a student navigates online daily is more complex than a checklist of don'ts. *How does a student's behavior online affect the overall community, and when do they have a moral obligation to act? When does student activism devolve into public shaming? How are a student's worldview and choices being impacted by an algorithm?* These are not black-and-white issues; they are thorny problems that require debate and self-discovery. By structuring *Ethics in a Digital World* with a Socratic form of questioning throughout the book, Dr. Mattson is providing you with terrific ways to stimulate classroom discussion and develop the critical thinking of your students. Furthermore, her presentation of major issues in the digital world, such as regulating misinformation, balancing user privacy with potential societal benefits, and determining whether artificial intelligence can reduce human bias, is rightly framed as claims that are currently being debated. Your students should be actively aware of this debate and able to have a depth of understanding to be an active participant in the debate as well.

Looking back at a tweet from Dr. Mattson from 2018, where she discussed developing "thoughtful, empathetic digital citizens who can wrestle with the important ethical questions at the intersection of technology and humanity," I want to emphasize the word *wrestle*. The issues found in *Ethics in a Digital World* are not merely to be understood but to be *wrestled* with. This is a major shift in how we typically approach "technology" topics, which are often oversimplified at a younger level. But learning how to be a digital citizen is far different from learning how to master Microsoft Excel. A student is both being affected by the digital world and affecting it. Unlike a relatively stable product that they can learn to use, the digital world is in a perpetual state of flux. This complexity necessitates a different type of student, one who can wrestle with issues instead of trying to memorize a set of ephemeral rules. To wrestle is to be actively engaged, and *Ethics in a Digital World* can help develop a generation that should not only thrive in the digital world but also actively work toward building a better one.

David Ryan Polgar is a pioneering tech ethicist, founder of All Tech Is Human, and a member of TikTok's Content Advisory Council. He previously co-founded the Digital Citizenship Summit, and he is an advocate for empowering students to be thoughtful digital citizens.

Introduction

In 2018, I wrote a tweet that is still pinned to my Twitter profile. It says that our definition of digital citizenship must expand beyond a list of digital missteps to avoid because what we really need are "thoughtful, empathetic digital citizens who can wrestle with the important ethical questions at the intersection of technology and humanity." I also asserted that "digital citizenship is the humanities curriculum of today and tomorrow."

As with most good ideas or aha moments, I cannot remember exactly how or why these words popped into my head one day, but when they formed, I knew I needed to get them out into the world. Two years later, I still go back to this tweet as I read about technology in schools and in the world, develop professional development and conference presentations, work with students and parents, and write about the topic of digital citizenship. Perhaps it is my background as an English teacher and school librarian that has colored my lenses this way, but I believe that digital citizenship belongs just as much in a humanities classroom as it does in a technology one.

When I wrote *Digital Citizenship in Action* for ISTE in 2017, my stance was considered progressive by many who had taught digital citizenship for years. I argued that instead of using digital citizenship curriculum as an attempt to correct or prevent misbehaviors online, we needed a proactive approach to equip students with the necessary skills to be active, engaged citizens in their digital communities. This shift meant encouraging educators to set aside the once-a-year assembly on cyberbullying, conduct purposeful work in classrooms year-round, and create opportunities for students to practice digital citizenship skills under the guidance of educators. The ideas presented in that book do not seem so radical anymore, thanks to the work of scholars, educators, and various organizations that have continued to redefine digital citizenship into something more meaningful than a behavior management curriculum. For example, a coalition of these organizations including ISTE and Common Sense Education, and for-profit companies in the edtech space like Google, Facebook, and NewsELA, have formed an initiative called DigCitCommit (digcitcommit.org). This partnership focuses on five competencies to shift the conversation from don'ts to do's: Inclusive, Informed, Engaged, Balanced, and Alert. Centered around these competencies, DigCitCommit strives to provide educators with resources that empower and engage students as digital citizens.

As I have watched an evolution in the conversation around digital citizenship education, schools have simultaneously been encouraged to step up their game in STEM (science, technology, engineering, and mathematics), even with our youngest learners. Educators have witnessed the rise of the Makerspace, Hour of Code, robotics kits in elementary classrooms, and professional development around design thinking and computation thinking. High schools across the country are adding electives in cybersecurity, game design, app development, and computer repair, as well as creating opportunities for students to earn recognized tech industry certifications before they graduate high school.

School curricula continue to adapt with an understanding that technology will play a huge part in the future of work. This progress is amazing. These steps are important. But because of who I am, my brain wonders what we might be missing, and I am always looking for the "what's next?" in education.

If we turn our eyes away from education toward the technology sector, we might have a possible answer to the "what's next?" question. More people are waking up to the notion that the technology they hold in their hands each day is not a neutral tool that individual users have ultimate control over. The facade began to publicly crack after accusations of Russian interference in the 2016 U.S. presidential election. The general public was introduced to the complexities of hacking, the concept of bot accounts, and the larger threat of information warfare. The rise in rhetoric around "fake news" has social media companies examining their role in the spread of misinformation, the public asking who checks the fact-checkers, and everyone from politicians to tech conglomerates wondering if, when, and how information regulation needs to happen.

I've spent the last few years reading up on the topic of tech ethics and exploring the human side of the digital tools that are all around us. My eyes have been opened to the amazing victories and unfortunate pitfalls of technology that I had never considered before. Each time I learned something new, I couldn't help but tuck it away into the "things we should be talking about with students" file folder in my brain. Eventually that file got so full, I could not help but begin a new book.

Writing a book like this, just as consuming a book like this, is not easy. It is not easy because there are no clear right or wrong answers to the ethical issues presented inside these pages. For each issue I ask you to examine, the pros and cons lists are equally long. So why bother to continue reading if you won't find answers to the questions presented within?

Well, in writing my learning down, my first intention is to help build your background knowledge on the various ethical issues being debated in the tech sector today. Once you have been exposed to these ideas, it is my hope that you—like me!—will feel inspired to engage the young digital citizens in your classrooms in conversations around these concepts. If you ascribe to the idea that technology is not neutral, if your students are already users of various technologies, and if you understand that many of our students will go on to make careers in a technology-related field, is it ever too soon to begin talking about the ethics of technology with them?

What Is in This Book

This book is divided into chapters based on six big ethical questions discussed in the technology sector and larger society today. Because each of these questions is so complex, I will be breaking them down by presenting you with:

- key vocabulary and definitions you and your students will come across in your investigation of each topic
- a short summary of the current research and viewpoints on the topic from leading experts in their fields

- news articles that serve as examples of the ethical questions playing out in society today (these articles can be easily accessed online and brought into your classroom for students to read)
- additional, focused research questions that students can use to explore the various aspects of the ethical dilemma
- stories of educators that are engaging students with lessons around tech ethics
- a "Try this" section with instructional strategies for helping students navigate open-ended questions
- QR codes that will link you to additional, curated content on each topic presented

Who This Book Is for

This book is written for middle and high school educators that are using technology with students in the classroom. It is not only for educators teaching skills like computational thinking, coding, design thinking, and problem solving, but it is also for educators who are not specifically tasked with teaching technology. The topics and questions presented in this book are perfect for teachers who specialize in the humanities—the English teacher, the social studies educator, the school librarian.

There can and should be an all-hands-on-deck approach to helping students consider the human side of the technology they use each day. There is not a single content area that should carry this burden alone, nor a single subject area that would struggle to find connections between these big questions and their content.

If you are ready to dive into the world of tech ethics, you have come to the right place! I cannot promise you'll find the answers to our current ethical dilemmas within these pages, but I can promise to educate you on the issues and help you find a way to talk about them with your students too.

Enjoy,
Kristen

Ethics in the Curriculum

Ethical conversation in the classroom is nothing new. Ethics, by the most basic definition, is the study and examination of the moral principles that govern a person's behavior. Our schools set and promote certain moral principles in mission statements, handbooks, school songs and pledges, and the chosen curriculum. Teachers, counselors, and administrators have ethical conversations with students when we attempt to understand the impetus for their choices or correct their misbehaviors.

Questions of humanity and morality come up in every novel we read. *To Kill a Mockingbird* forces us to examine where community standards end and the individual rights begin, as well as how we must wrestle with our own personal beliefs when they come into conflict with our community's ethical codes. In *Lord of the Flies*, we must confront two instincts that live within man—one that is completely self-centered and seeks only to satisfy his own needs, and another instinct to follow a set of rules and values so we can live in peaceful community with others. As teachers guide students through these and countless other novels that deal with morality, they are helping students examine their own ethical codes and belief systems too.

Just as novels can be a vehicle for helping students examine their personal morals, our government, sociology, and psychology courses help students wrestle with ethics through a larger, societal lens. Controversial topics such as privacy, censorship, the death penalty, and minimum wage are often analyzed through current events, prior Supreme Court rulings, and the impact of decisions on large groups of the population. Humanities teachers are not the only ones having ethical conversations in the classroom. Science and math teachers frequently talk about the professional ethics that guide work in data collection, experimentation, ecology, astronomy, medicine, and more.

As technology becomes a greater part of our society, educators must consider the role that innovation, global connectedness, and unlimited access to information play on the moral and ethical underpinnings of society that we have long discussed with students. How is technology changing our culture? How is innovation making us question aspects of our society that we may not have before? And whose ethical and moral principles will guide future innovation, lawmaking, and community living?

Frameworks to Situate Digital Ethics Amongst Other Ethical Questions

Digital ethics, also referred to as tech ethics, are a unique set of ethical dilemmas that can be examined through a variety of frameworks. In the same way that people approach social issues such as gun control or personal issues such as marriage infidelity from different perspectives and viewpoints, individuals will bring their varied backgrounds, experiences, and belief systems into conversations around tech ethics.

It is not vital for your students to understand all these frameworks in depth, but you may find it helpful to familiarize yourself with them. Understanding the various groundworks from which people approach ethical thinking can help you be a more empathetic guide and aid you in helping students see various perspectives too.

Let's examine five ethical theories that have served as a guide to philosophers and scholars over time:

1. Virtue Ethics – This ethical theory, typically associated with Aristotle, emphasizes the importance of developing and refining an individual's character rather than developing and reinforcing a strict set of societal rules. Virtue ethics argues that if we can focus on being good people, the right actions will effortlessly

follow. Therefore, our goal as humans is to be as virtuous as possible.

2. Natural Law Ethics – This ethical theory, often credited to Thomas Aquinas, forwards the idea that God created man with natural inclinations toward things that are good, such as avoiding danger or ensuring the reproduction of the species. Aquinas believed that ethical standards have their ultimate origin in God's divine plan for humanity.

3. Social Contract Ethics – Thomas Hobbes forwarded the idea that there are more benefits to living under social contract with one another than living in a society of no rules to govern our collective behaviors. "Right" acts are ones that do not violate the implicit and explicit agreements that we have made with one another as humans in community.

4. Utilitarian Ethics – Founded by Jeremy Bentham, this moral theory focuses on the results, or consequences, of our actions and treats our intentions as irrelevant. Actions should be measured in terms of the happiness or pleasure they produce, and humans should act in ways that always produce the greatest good for the greatest number of people.

5. Deontological Ethics – Immanuel Kant's theory of ethics is the most popular example of deontological thinking. He argued that it was not the consequences of one's actions that made them right or wrong, but the motives of the person who carried it out. We can only evaluate the will or character of a person based on his or her motives and intentions (Mizzoni, 2017).

Consider how a typical digital citizenship topic like cyberbullying could be taught depending upon the ethical frameworks we, or our communities, ascribe to:

- Virtue Ethics: Be the absolute best person you can be online. If everyone acts with kindness, cyberbullying will disappear.

Vocabulary to Know

Ethics – the study and examination of moral principles that guide some-one's behavior; standards of "good and bad" or "right and wrong" at a community or societal level.

Morals – a personal guide to behavior; the ways you determine "good and bad" or "right and wrong." Your morals may align with or contradict the ethics of your community.

Digital Ethics / Tech Ethics – terms often used interchangeably to describe a field of study that seeks to understand and resolve ethical issues surrounding the development and use of various digital applications.

Personal Digital Ethics – the standards that guide one's conduct and decision-making in digital settings.

Ethical Frameworks – value systems that individuals or groups use to guide their behavior. Many philosophers have forwarded their ideas about how society comes to decide what is "good and bad." Only a few of them are presented in this book.

- Natural Law Ethics: You know right from wrong, kids. You were born with a moral compass and cyberbullying is not okay. Trust your gut. If something feels wrong, you should not do it.

- Social Contract Ethics: Our digital communities can be much better places if we all agree to abide by a certain code of ethics. You can help create those expectations and uphold them by calling out others who cyberbully and letting them know their actions are not welcome.

- Utilitarian Ethics: Your words were hurtful to me. I don't care if you were joking. I don't care if you didn't mean it. The way I feel because of your bullying behavior is more important than why you did it.

- Deontological Ethics: Cyberbullying is awful, but we must re-member that not everyone intends to hurt others with their words. Some people have only been taught one way to commu-nicate or were raised in a home with bad role models. We must seek to understand the person and the intentions behind the actions.

One way to challenge students is to have them view the topics presented in this book through these five different ethical frameworks. Help them consider how the ethical questions and possible solutions change when we take a new perspective or set of ethical values.

Why Engage Students in Conversations of Tech Ethics?

There are many reasons to engage students in conversations around tech ethics. Not only are they consumers of technology, but they also use tech-nology as a vital piece of their interpersonal relationships, their source for gathering information, and their connection to the greater society. In addi-tion, students are already producers of content and may eventually become the creators of major platforms, software, algorithms, technical products, and services. Rather than being mindless consumers or producers, we want our students to be critical thinkers—which is something that ethical con-versations require students to do.

Tech ethics for consumers and producers

In considering the roles students play as technology users and consumers, we may encourage them to think about their *personal digital ethics*. Most digi-tal citizenship curricula encourage students to develop their personal ethics as it relates to technology. In developing personal digital ethics for yourself or for your children, you may have thought through questions such as:

- Is it okay to post pictures of someone without their permission? Does this apply to parents posting pictures of their infant chil-dren since infants cannot give consent?

- Who can my child interact with online? How will those rules change as my child gets older and more mature?

- How will I interact with others when I am online? Does this code of conduct I have created for myself apply in every situation?

Digital citizenship curriculum makes attempts at furthering a social contract through lessons on social media etiquette, digital friendships, cyberbullying, and hate speech. But as the distance between us continues to shrink via the internet, it is becoming clearer that not everyone lives by the same social contract and that our ethical systems are not as universal as once thought.

You can help students more thoroughly examine their personal digital ethics through some of the ethical frameworks that were presented earlier in this chapter. When we feel slighted online, for example, are we more concerned about the intention of the person who slighted us or the consequences that came from it? When we make a choice to speak online against an injustice, are we doing so to signal our own virtues or as an attempt to create the greatest good for the greatest number of people?

This book is less about our personal digital ethics, though, and more about technology ethics—the process of asking how we can apply ethical thinking to the design and development of new technologies and the refinement of existing ones. Understanding the morals that guide our individual technology use, however, can help us unpack our thoughts and feelings around the larger questions that are presented in the following chapters.

Tech ethics and social and emotional learning (SEL)

Conversations about all types of ethical issues, technological ones included, can support students' social and emotional development. CASEL, the Collaborative for Academic, Social, and Emotional Learning, reports that social and emotional learning (SEL) "enhances students' capacity to integrate skills, attitudes, and behaviors to deal effectively and ethically with daily tasks and challenges" (2020).

The CASEL Core SEL Competencies state that students should be continuously working on the following:

- Self-awareness: the ability to accurately recognize one's own emotions, thoughts, and values

- Self-management: the ability to regulate one's emotions, thoughts, and behaviors in different situations

- Social awareness: the ability to take the perspective of and empathize with others and to understand social and ethical norms for behavior

- Relationship skills: the ability to communicate clearly, cooperate, listen well, and negotiate conflict

- Responsible decision-making: the ability to make constructive choices about personal behavior and social interactions based on ethical standards and social norms

In just about every competency of social and emotional learning, students are asked to metacognitively consider and act upon ethical standards. They can only do so if they have opportunities for practice. Speaking about tech ethics with students is just one more chance for them to consider various perspectives and the impact technology has on us as individuals and as a society.

Tech ethics and the ISTE Standards

The ISTE Standards for Students are "designed to empower student voice and ensure that learning is a student-driven process" (ISTE, 2016). The ISTE Standards for Educators are a "road map to helping students become empowered learners. These standards will deepen your practice, promote collaboration with peers, challenge you to rethink traditional approaches and prepare students to drive their own learning" (ISTE, 2017). Many schools and educational institutions around the globe look to the ISTE Standards to guide the integration of technology into the curriculum.

There are several ISTE Standards for Students and ISTE Standards for Educators indicators that implore us to examine not only the possibilities of innovation but also the human responsibilities that come with both using and designing various technology solutions. To help illustrate the connection between the ideas in this book and the ISTE Standards, I have included the relevant standards that pertain to the "Try this" and "Curricular Connections" sections in each chapter. As you consider adding conversations of technology ethics into your classes, apply these standards alongside content area standards to re-create powerful learning goals and instructional targets.

 To view the ISTE Standards for Students in full, scan the QR code.

 To view the ISTE Standards for Educators in full, scan the QR code.

Tips for Successful Discussions

Watching freshman in a social studies or English class participate in their very first Socratic seminar of the year is always a little awkward. The seniors are typically pros by the time they leave our building, and observing how students progress over four years is evidence that academic discussion needs to be taught and practiced, just like any other skill!

A Socratic seminar is just one of many discussion protocols that can be used in the classroom. They are typically based on a text or set of texts and an open-ended question. During the discussion, students must listen closely to their peers, think critically about what they have read and are hearing, and articulate their own thoughts in response to the thoughts of others (Israel, 2002).

The first few Socratic seminars of the school year are typically awkward because students are not used to this type of discussion format. Occasionally, teachers rush through the preparation phase, not taking the proper time to model or practice the art of text-based discussion. Students also approach their first few seminars without having read enough material to develop background knowledge or come across opposing viewpoints. This can happen when teachers require students to bring an article or two into the discussion with little guidance on how to choose a quality text. Students also come timidly into the conversation because they may not know everyone in their class, have fears about public speaking, or do not feel comfortable with or informed enough about the topic. Pair all the aforementioned issues with the pressure of a good grade and it's no wonder the first few Socratic seminars are painful to watch.

You can avoid some of the common missteps I have seen in Socratic seminars at the start of the year by taking more time to prepare students for successful discussions. As with any other skill, how to discuss multifaceted ethical issues is one that must be taught. In addition to a lot of practice, grace, and feedback during the conversations, there is a lot of work that must happen before students even sit down to a formal discussion.

Teach the process of ethical thinking

The Markkula Center for Applied Ethics at Santa Clara University in California is one of the leaders in bringing "ethical thinking to bear on real world problems" (Markkula, n.d.). The Center serves professionals in a variety of fields, including business, medicine, technology, education, and government. Members of the staff believe that ethics can be taught, and they provide a simple framework to help people think through an ethical issue. I have summarized the steps here in student-friendly language and have elaborated on each one to help you implement them in your classes.

Step one: Recognize an ethical issue

Before we ask students to weigh the pros and cons of any ethical issue, we must help them recognize where ethical issues exist. This book is intended to help highlight ethical issues in the technology that surrounds us by putting them in plain language for you and your students, but these topics are not the only ones that can help students begin to think ethically.

You can help students recognize ethical issues by bringing current events into the classroom. As I am writing, the world is trying to decide how to get students back to school amidst COVID-19. There are all types of ethical issues in these discussions, which is what makes them difficult. Do we prioritize face-to-face learning more than public safety? Who "wins" and who "loses" if we stick with remote learning? Are we prepared to handle the outcomes of any of our options? Any time there are tough choices to be made, there are ethical issues to be brought to light.

By presenting the topics in this book (as well as other ethical dilemmas) to your students, they will become more prone to look for and recognize ethical issues on their own.

Step two: Get the facts

It is difficult to debate the pros and cons of any issue, decision, or technology without background knowledge. This book is designed to equip you with just that—from important vocabulary, history, and context to summaries of research and current news stories. Think of the chapter structure of this book as a guide for the type of background knowledge you will want to equip your students with as they move through the ethical decision-making process.

Step three: Explore various options

Our gut reaction is to pick a side and stick with it, but it is important that we explore not only options that have already been presented but also brainstorm options we may not have considered yet. Get students in the habit of asking "what if?" and "what about?" and "why is it that way?"

There are several reasons this book presents more than one argument for each topic discussed:

1. Presenting only one argument may lead readers to believe I have all the answers, which I do not. Each of these ethical dilemmas is complex and has many gray areas.

2. To intelligently discuss an ethical dilemma, we must understand more than one perspective and be open to learning about

additional perspectives we may not have considered yet. Before making a recommendation or deciding how to act, it is best to have more information, not less.

3. Without seeing multiple perspectives, it is difficult to grasp why a dilemma even exists.

Step four: Make a decision and test it

In a school setting, this is not as easy as it would be if our students were in the field, creating technology products. So we must get creative in how we get our students to test their theories. We can encourage them to think through their recommendation by asking:

1. What is the worst-case scenario?
2. What is the best-case scenario?
3. What does a random sampling of actual users have to say?
4. What do our parents, teachers, or other adults think?
5. Who "wins" with this decision and who "loses"?

Step five: Reflect on the outcome

After talking with others, making pros and cons lists, and looking for examples that answer the "what if?" questions, students can make better recommendations for how to make a product or process better for a given audience.

Focus discussion through various lenses

It can be easy for us to think about the personal impacts of a new technology, but it can be a little more difficult to think about the broader, societal impacts. You can help students have more nuanced conversations by introducing various lenses into the conversation through the questions you pose. Here are a few angles we can take when discussing an issue of technology ethics.

Social lens

1. Does this technology foster or undermine a sense of community?
2. Does the technology empower community members?
3. What is the effect of this technology on relationships?
4. Does it affect our way of seeing or experiencing the world?
5. Does it erase a sense of time and history?
6. How might this innovation uphold or adhere to democratic principles?

Moral lens

1. What values does this technology foster?
2. Whose values are acknowledged? Whose values may have been ignored?
3. What problems does this innovation allow society to ignore?
4. How does this impact the least advantaged in society?
5. Are we able to assume personal and/or community responsibility for the effect?

Knowledge and vocation

1. Does this reduce, deaden, or enhance human creativity?
2. Does it build on, or contribute to, the renewal of traditional forms of knowledge? Does it replace, or does it aid, human hands and human beings?
3. What is its impact on craft?
4. Does it foster a diversity of forms of knowledge?
5. Does it create or reduce opportunities for employment and economic growth?

Health and wellness

1. What is this technology's potential to become addictive?
2. Are there concerns about side effects or long-term health issues?
3. What are the possible impacts on mental health?

4. Will this lead to better overall health?
5. Will this add or remove barriers to quality healthcare for all?

Environment

1. What is the environmental impact to produce this product?
2. How will the disposal of this product impact the health of the planet?
3. In what ways can this product influence a greener economy?
4. How might the environmental impacts of this technology affect future generations?

Utilize discussion protocols

We cannot simply ask students to "discuss"; there must be guided protocols in place to help bring all students into the conversation. The Socratic seminar is just one example of a discussion structure that is used in classrooms today. At the end of each chapter in the "Try this" section, you will find example activities and discussion protocols that can help you engage your students in these ethical conversations. Even though the "Try this" activity is featured alongside a specific ethical issue, you can certainly mix and match the protocols with different topics as you see fit.

Give ample time, resources, modeling, and feedback

If students are expected to examine the issues presented in these pages, you will need to provide them with proper resources to build background knowledge. Utilize the news articles featured in this book and the additional resources that have been curated and linked to via QR codes at the end of each chapter. Reach out to your school or local librarian to help you find additional high-quality sources. If you want to encourage students to find their own information to bring to the discussion, make sure you have minimally given each student the same, equal foundation of background knowledge first.

To have a great discussion, students need time and feedback during the research and background building process as well. Preview student notes prior to the discussion. Identify where there are gaps in their thinking and send them back to the knowledge-building phase. Prepare students for discussion by providing graphic organizers to help outline the pros and cons of various viewpoints.

During a discussion, take notes on what the class did well and where they can improve. Consider writing a "letter to the class" where you outline the strengths and weaknesses of the discussion as a whole and have students write a personal reflection on their own performance based on your whole group feedback. Then add direct instruction on areas where the entire class could use support—crafting better arguments, providing stronger evidence, or even ways to include more voices into the conversation.

Onward!

As you move through the following chapters, my hope is that you can grow in your own understanding of the ethical issues surrounding technology today. More than that, though, as my 2018 tweet suggests, I hope that you will feel inspired to help students develop into "thoughtful, empathetic digital citizens who can wrestle with the important ethical questions at the intersection of technology and humanity."

Access to Information: Is It Time to Better Regulate the Internet?

In December of 2016, Edgar Maddison Welch walked into a Washington, D.C., pizza restaurant called Comet Ping Pong with a semiautomatic rifle, a handgun, and a pocketknife. He was not there to pick up dinner for his family. He was on a mission to save sexually abused children who were being held in the basement of the pizza place. Before the mission, Welch tried to persuade a few friends to help him, but when they declined, he decided to continue on his own.

Upon entering the restaurant, Welch did not find any children, even after strolling through the back and shooting the lock off a cabinet filled with cooking supplies so he could get a look inside. He couldn't find the basement either—probably because Comet Ping Pong didn't have one.

No, Welch was not mentally unstable. He was not confused about the location or what he thought he would find there. He felt compelled to act after hearing Alex Jones, an alt-right radio show host and conspiracy theorist, report that Hillary Clinton was running a pedophile ring out of the Comet Ping Pong basement. Welch also saw similar reports on Breitbart News and recalled seeing the story shared on various social media sites.

Following Welch's arrest, several media outlets started tracing the origins of the pedophile-ring story that came to be known as #Pizzagate. Although the first explicitly detailed outline of the conspiracy theory appears to have been a Facebook post by a sixty-year-old woman in Missouri, investigators found "seeds" of information on various 4chan and Reddit boards. It is still unclear whether #Pizzagate was concocted through mass hysteria or if it was the work of real political players with resources and an agenda. Either way, the arrest of Edgar Maddison Welch made it clear that "fake news" can have very real consequences (Robb, 2017).

There are no clear answers to the problems we face with disinformation, hate speech, misogyny, and racism on the internet, but this chapter will give you and your students a starting point to begin a discussion around the following questions:

- Should there be more concentrated efforts to regulate misinformation and disinformation online?

- Who should be our digital content monitors? Who should be responsible for protecting users from hate speech, threats, or other harmful content?

- Where might regulation cross the line and interfere with freedom of speech?

Building Background Knowledge

Being an information-literate person during a time of rampant misinformation spread can be exhausting! But when we talk about regulating the internet, the discussion around fake news or misinformation is just the tip of the iceberg.

For years, there has been debate over whether we owe it to children to censor specific content, such as pornography, on the internet. There have been debates over net neutrality and whether the internet should be free and open or if internet service providers should be able to charge companies a premium to deliver content faster than a competitor. People argue whether an online threat should be viewed in the same way as a face-to-face one or if the people on the receiving end are just thin-skinned and cannot handle a troll. And finally, people argue about who—if anyone—should be regulating the digital "wild west."

Vocabulary to Know

Misinformation – typically describes falsehoods that are spread either purposely or accidentally; satire is a purposeful form of misinformation, whereas a journalist's mistake would be an accidental one.

Disinformation – refers to information specifically designed to deceive or mislead; it includes fake news, propaganda, manipulated images or video, and more.

Fake News – factually inaccurate information designed to appear like legitimate news; a form of disinformation.

Filter Bubble – users are said to be in a filter bubble when they only encounter information and opinions that reinforce their own beliefs. This phenomenon is caused by algorithms that deliver users more of the same content they already consume.

Echo Chambers – echo chambers are similar to filter bubbles in that users only encounter information and opinions that coincide with their own. An echo chamber, though, is self-created based on the accounts and groups one chooses to follow.

Hate Speech – public speech that expresses hate or encourages violence toward people or groups of people based on qualities such as race, religion, ability, gender expression, or sexual orientation.

The next few sections will give you important background to know and consider when asking, is it time to better regulate content on the internet?

The conundrum of mis- and disinformation

Misinformation has been defined as untrue information that spreads either purposely or accidentally. Satirical newspapers like *The Onion* present information that is not intended to be factual but often mirrors phenomena that are occurring in the world in an exaggerated way. This is an example of purposeful misinformation, designed to entertain or make us think about a topic from a different angle. Unfortunately, not everyone can differentiate satire from fact, and some may confuse satirical writing with truth.

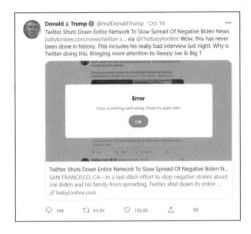

This was the case in October 2020 when President Donald Trump retweeted an article from the satirical news site The Babylon Bee (Trump, 2020). The article he shared claimed that Twitter shut down its entire platform to keep negative information about his oppo-

Figure 2.1 President Donald Trump mistakes satire for fact.

nent Joe Biden from spreading. Babylon Bee wrote the satirical headline just hours after Twitter temporarily experienced technical difficulties that kept users from posting.

The Babylon Bee article is an example of purposeful misinformation. However, a journalist mistakenly reporting a false detail in a story or a President sharing satire as truth would be examples of accidental misinformation, and any credible journalist, news organization, or elected official should be transparent in correcting such errors.

Disinformation, on the other hand, is purposefully designed to fool or sway people by presenting distorted facts or outright lies as absolute truths. Examples of disinformation include the following: a Photoshopped image designed to make a politician or celebrity look bad, a viral video in which someone poses as a doctor and offers medical advice, a far-right or far-left "news" organization that publishes only sensationalized rumors and conspiracy theories. When people use the term *fake news*, they are referring to a form of disinformation. Misinformation and disinformation are certainly a problem on the internet, but they do not exist as a singular evil inside of a vacuum. They are only one part of the much larger picture of what is happening online today.

Disinformation gets perpetuated for several reasons. First, bias is not just written into the things we consume. We approach information with a bias as readers too. One bias that is incredibly hard to fight is *anchoring bias*. When individuals depend heavily on the first piece of information they see on a topic (the "anchor"), it becomes the foundation with which new information, arguments, and viewpoints are negotiated. When disinformation is the anchor, it can be hard for people to reconcile contrary—even factual—ideas they encounter.

A second type of bias that helps perpetuate disinformation is *confirmation bias*. With confirmation bias, we tend to weigh evidence that confirms our beliefs more heavily than evidence that goes against our beliefs. Disinformation can be more tempting to grab onto than facts if the ideas help confirm what we believe to be true.

Aside from the personal biases that cause us to double down on what we believe to be true (even if it isn't!), filter bubbles can perpetuate the sharing of disinformation as well. The term *filter bubble* describes the environment we find ourselves in when the algorithms designed to personalize content for us end up trapping us in a "bubble" of one-sided information. "Like" more of your liberal friends' posts on Facebook? You will see more of their posts than the posts of your conservative friends. Tend to click on Fox News more than CNN in a Google search? Fox News will appear at the top of your results list. While personalization can be helpful when it comes to entertainment platforms like Netflix, it can be dangerous if we are inadvertently feeding ourselves a steady diet of disinformation.

The last way disinformation is perpetuated is through echo chambers. *Echo chambers* are a lot like filter bubbles, but they are self-created, not algorithmically driven. When we choose voices to follow on Twitter that mirror ours only or join Facebook groups based on the common ground we have with others on a singular viewpoint, we have created an echo chamber where no one challenges our ideas or assumptions, and we are not often exposed to ideals other than our own.

These echo chambers can be a powerful place for disinformation to spread.

> These effects [of bias, misinformation, and echo chambers] are interrelated, creating a feedback loop that could damage democracy. Low-information voters, kept uninformed by falsehoods and narratives of false equivalencies, harden their political biases by selecting media that confirm their previous beliefs, regardless of whether those media report true or fake stories. This increases polarization, which both erodes trust in traditional reporting and further encourages selection of confirming media. Fake news is a self-reinforcing problem. (Waldman, 2018, p. 851)

If fake news truly is a self-reinforcing problem that individuals themselves are unable to break away from, it further begs the question, "is it time to better regulate the internet?"

Platforms for hate

Reddit. 4chan. YouTube. Three of many social media spaces that at one time or another have been labeled as a "platform for hate." 4chan critics claim the anonymity in the space is the perfect petri dish for growing hate speech, conspiracy theories, and acts of violence. An analysis of 1 million comments on a single 4chan board called "Politically Incorrect" revealed a 40% increase in racial, ethnic, and religious slurs between 2015 and 2019. Comments that paired hate speech with threats of violence against minority communities increased by 25% in the same four-year window (Arthur, 2019). 4chan is not the only online space where hate speech has had a place to take hold, though.

Reddit first launched as a site in 2005 but only recently instated a ban on hate speech. Although Reddit made some attempts to clean up the website in 2015 with the removal of several racist forums such as "Coontown," their policies did not explicitly ban all racist and hate-filled forums and posts. The June 2020 update to Reddit policies resulted in the removal of 2,000 subreddits, including one called "The_Donald," which had nearly 800,000 active members and was littered with misogynistic, anti-Semitic, racist, and anti-Muslim content (Spangler, 2020). Many applaud Reddit's recent efforts to free the space of harassment, bullying, and hate-filled threats, but critics say the company's efforts are too little too late.

Finally, YouTube is another company struggling to decide what types of content to allow on its platform. In June 2019, YouTube updated its hate-speech policy to include a ban on supremacist content and content that denied major events such as the Holocaust, 9/11, or the 2012 Sandy Hook school shooting. During a three-month window following the update, YouTube removed more than 100,000 videos, 17,000 channels, and 500 million comments over hate speech. Critics, including the Anti-Defamation League, say that YouTube still hasn't done enough (Yurieff, 2019a). In fact, it took YouTube more than a year to decide to remove six high-profile white supremacists from the platform, including former KKK leader David Duke (Yurieff, 2020).

Hate speech, conspiracy theories, misogyny, and racism run rampant online despite efforts by social media companies to curb it. Is this just part of the price we pay in a global society, or is there more that can be done to make the internet a space that is safe for all?

A threatened democracy

Harvard government professors and authors Steven Levitsky and Daniel Ziblatt speak about the breakdown of democracies around the world, including the United States, in their 2018 book *How Democracies Die*. They claim that "the weakening of our democratic norms is rooted in extreme partisan polarization—one that extends beyond policy differences into an existential conflict over race and culture . . . and if one thing is clear from studying breakdowns throughout history, it's that extreme polarization can kill democracies" (9).

Misinformation, disinformation, our personal biases, and our social media echo chambers have all contributed to the extreme polarization we see in the United States today. However, it is becoming clear that decisions made behind the scenes of major social media platforms are also a contributing factor. Aside from the issues of hate speech and supremacist content that were mentioned above, companies like Facebook have been called to address even bigger issues on their platforms.

In the last few years, Facebook founder and CEO Mark Zuckerberg has appeared in front of the United States Congress on more than one occasion.

Lawmakers have grilled Zuckerberg on everything from the possibility of Russian meddling in the 2016 election through Facebook to the possibility that the company is censoring more conservative viewpoints. Zuckerberg has faced criticism over security breaches that resulted in the harvesting and selling of users' political profiles to Cambridge Analytica, a political consulting firm. The company has also been criticized for its refusal to fact-check political advertisements (*The New York Times*, 2018).

It is difficult to deny the role that social media platforms play in global politics. The question is whether we can harness them for good or if they will cause such polarization that the U.S. democracy will not be able to withstand the strain.

Now that you understand some of the more pressing issues that exist around online content, the question is, what (if anything) can we do to solve those concerns?

Breaking Down the Arguments

I was browsing around the Google Chrome Extensions store one day when I came across a Trump Filter for Chrome. The extension was "presented as part of the antidote for [Trump's] toxic candidacy. This Chrome extension will identify parts of a web page likely to contain Donald Trump and erase them from the Internet" (Spectre, 2017). Of course, I had to install the extension and see for myself what this thing could do.

At first, the extension made me laugh. I conducted a Google Images search for U.S. Presidents and then slowly watched images of Donald Trump magically disappear from my results list. A search for presidential speeches turned up a small number of results, but none of them were from President Trump.

After playing around with the extension for a while, I did a search for "covid 19" and literally watched more than 5 billion results disappear. All that remained was a map and a few charts of recent cases from the CDC (Figure 2.1). Apparently, the odds of President Trump appearing in coronavirus-related news were so high that the extension blocked almost every single one. I uninstalled the Trump Filter (Figure 2.2) but found myself lingering

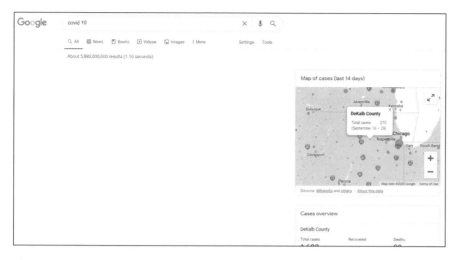

Figure 2.2 Google search results for "covid 19" when using the Trump Filter Chrome extension

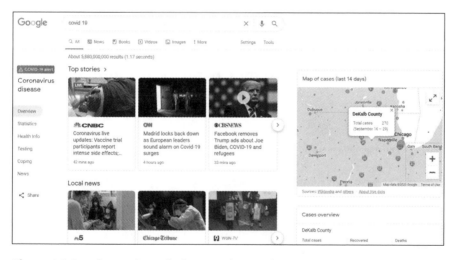

Figure 2.3 Google search results for "covid 19" without the Trump Filter Chrome extension

over it all evening. Even if the Trump Filter was created to be a joke, I kept coming back to the question, "What dangers exist when we choose to ignore (rather than engage with) people, media channels, political issues, or scientific data that does not align with our personal convictions?"

As adults, should we be able to completely ignore entire political parties, news networks, social groups, and unpopular opinions with just a few clicks of the mouse? On the opposite side of the coin, what obligation do we have to fellow internet users when we choose what to share? Should we be able to freely share misinformation or conspiracy theories simply because *we* believe them? Is it okay for us to pass along videos of sexual assault, suicide, or police brutality that may be triggering to large groups of our society? Should that type of content even be allowed to exist on the internet in the first place? Who gets to decide?

In the next few sections, I will outline three major claims about who should be regulating our internet. I will highlight expert voices in the field and provide relevant, timely examples that appear in the headlines. The original research can help you better understand the topic, but it can also be summarized for students when introducing the ethical problem to the class. News articles can be used to build student background knowledge, support their research projects, or be injected into classroom conversations to highlight the complexities of the topic.

Claim #1: Government should regulate disinformation online.

Individuals who take this stance are likely to support their viewpoint through these assertions:

- Government regulation protects consumers from being cheated or manipulated.

- Social media companies were built on platforms designed around profit and popularity, not truth. Only government regulation and consequences for not complying can force companies to change.

- The United States democracy could be at stake if we do not control misinformation. It is the job of the government to protect our democracy.

What the research says

Most Americans who disagree with government regulation of misinformation on the internet will argue that the First Amendment protects their freedom of speech, and what people choose to publish on the internet should also be protected from oversight by any governing body. In this section, however, we will unpack what a few legal experts say regarding the role regulation might play in fighting misinformation online.

One option the U.S. government may have for curbing dangerous disinformation is to regulate it in the same ways they regulate commercial speech. Traditionally, speech receives the highest levels of constitutional protection under the First Amendment, but courts allow for much more scrutiny and regulation of commercial speech because its sole purpose is to persuade consumers to purchase goods.

One example where this type of commercial regulation might work well is in the case of a Los Angeles–based company called Disinfomedia. Disinfomedia owns many fake news domains, including the "Denver Guardian," and has employed up to twenty-five writers at a time to churn out clickbait. The founder and CEO, Jestin Coler, claims his company can make upwards of $30,000 a month by simply writing sensational stories and sprinkling them around social media (Sydell, 2016).

Because Disinformedia makes money based on traffic to their site, the enticing headlines are technically commercial advertisements inviting consumers to click, read, and share content—all of which helps the company turn a profit. Lawyers argue that courts may be more compelled to regulate disinformation online, even under the First Amendment, if they are willing to recognize that groups producing clickbait-y content are not trying to engage in political discourse, but are actually pursuing a "commercial enterprise where fake news is a sellable commodity" (Andorfer, 2018, p. 1425).

In that same regard, the government could step in and regulate free speech from the perspective of consumer protections. Even though we do not pay for fake news directly, the sites profit by collecting our data (which can be sold) and by racking up high traffic, clicks, and shares that result in advertising revenue. The Federal Trade Commission (FTC) is an agency dedicated to protecting consumers from unfair and/or deceptive business practices. The FTC has challenged all types of deceptive practices, from misleading advertisements to deceptive product demonstrations—both of which can make it difficult for a consumer to decide if a product is one of quality or if it is a "lemon." The FTC has already moved against some websites that exist solely to pump out fake reviews about real products. This precedent might allow the FTC to further regulate fake news and "fake news factories" in the future to protect consumers from scams, fraud, and other types of harmful forms of misinformation (Waldman, 2018).

In the news

FTC Seeks to Halt 10 Operators of Fake News Sites from Making Deceptive Claims about Acai Berry Weight Loss Products (FTC, 2011)

The Federal Trade Commission requests that federal courts halt the operations of ten fake news websites that are nothing more than advertisements marketing acai berry weight-loss products. The complaint alleges that the sites are using deceptive titles like "News 6 News Alerts" and often include the names and logos of legitimate media outlets such as *USA Today* and Consumer Reports. The FTC is requesting refunds for consumers who purchased products from these blatantly misleading websites.

NY Attorney General Targets Fake Social Media Activity (Jones, 2019)

New York Attorney General Letitia James settled a case with a company called Devumi that sold fake followers, "likes," comments, and views on social media platforms such as Twitter, YouTube, LinkedIn, and Sound-Cloud. The company earned approximately $15 million selling fake social media activity to clients that included athletes, actresses, influencers, and entrepreneurs. This social media activity came from bots and other fake accounts. Attorney General James said, "With this settlement, we are sending a clear message that anyone profiting off of deception and impersonation is breaking the law and will be held accountable."

Claim #2: Community-based regulation is better than internet rules.

The "Trump Filter" extension is just one example of user-created, community-based internet regulation. Individuals who believe the internet is best regulated by the people who use it are likely to support their viewpoint with assertions such as:

- Historical attempts by governments to regulate the internet have not gone well.
- Government regulation could easily cross a line into censorship.
- Media literacy education is the answer to misinformation.

What the research says

In a 2019 study from Princeton University, researchers Pennycook and Rand suggest there is promise in fighting misinformation through crowdsourcing. One way to fight "fake news" would be to train algorithms to up-rank content from trusted media outlets on social media platforms. But to train an algorithm, you need a dataset. And what better way to get a dataset than to crowdsource one?

In an effort to determine if crowdsourcing the data was a viable approach, the Princeton researchers ran two separate experiments to see where individuals rated their familiarity with and their trust in sixty different web-domains from three categories: mainstream media outlets, hyper-partisan websites, and websites that produce blatantly false content. Even though there were substantial political differences in both the participants and the news sources they were asked to rank, the researchers found that laypeople rated mainstream sources as far more reputable than either hyper-partisan or fake news sites. While some sub-groups were slightly better at the task than others, the group in its entirety was in remarkably high agreement with professional fact-checkers (Pennycook & Rand, 2019).

The results of this study suggest that our collective intelligence might be better than any government regulation or tech solution at identifying quality sources of news sources. Other scholars agree that disinformation on the internet is not a problem that will be solved by tech companies or governing bodies but by people themselves.

In the summer of 2017, Pew Research Center interviewed more than 1,100 technologists, scholars, and practitioners and asked if the information environment would or would not improve in the next ten years. The replies were nearly split down the middle with 49% of respondents feeling hopeful about the future of the information landscape and 51% responding that the environment would not improve. Those that were optimistic did not credit their hopes to technology or government interference, though. Instead, those with a positive view of the future of information noted that humans, over time, will become more adept at sorting through material, that crowdsourcing will work to highlight verified facts and block lies and propaganda, and that information literacy will become a more pressing goal at all levels of education (Anderson & Rainie, 2017).

In the news

Twitter is Testing New Ways to Fight Misinformation—Including a Community-Based Points System (Collins, 2020)

Twitter is experimenting with a feature that adds bright red and orange badges to tweets that have been reported by users as harmfully misleading. Twitter's priority would be to start labeling the tweets of politicians and other public figures with large numbers of followers before expanding the feature. In the same way that users of Wikipedia can challenge and correct misinformation, Twitter envisions using a "community reports" feature to help fact-checkers, journalists, and other verified moderator accounts provide more critical context, research, and even opposing arguments underneath the original, flagged tweets. This is just one more example of a technology company relying on the collective knowledge of its digital citizens to improve the community for everyone.

K-pop Stans Take over Racist Hashtags on Twitter (Morse & Wong, 2020)

After the May 2020 death of George Floyd at the hands of Minneapolis police, #BlackLivesMatter protests erupted around the country and on social media. Unfortunately, counter-protest and white supremacist hashtags like #WhiteLivesMatter and #WhiteOutWednesday began trending on Twitter as well. It did not take long, though, for K-pop (Korean pop music) artists and fans to drown out the white supremacist hashtags with images, videos, and GIFs of their favorite K-pop bands. K-pop fans also took to Instagram to take over the hashtags. Anyone who clicked on the trending hashtags saw nothing but amazing K-pop content! This is just one example of how a digital community can come together to drown out hate speech online.

Claim #3: Tech companies are best equipped to handle misinformation on their platforms.

Individuals who take this stance are likely to support their viewpoint through the following assertions:

- Tech companies have created this wild west; it is up to them to clean it up.

- Tech companies have made billions of dollars off of consumers. They can afford to improve their algorithms, employ more content monitors, and enforce their codes of conduct.

- Tech companies should partner with third-party regulators to ensure neutral application of a platform's codes of conduct.

What the research says

Fact-checking and content moderation is not a new concept for social media giants like Facebook and Twitter. In 2014, there were 44 active fact-checking initiatives on record, but that number has quadrupled in the past five years to 194 active fact-checking projects in more than sixty countries. Tech giants like Google offer grant funding to organizations that might bolster and expand automated fact-checking solutions.

Artificial intelligence (AI) solutions have proven highly effective in the removal of bot accounts and illegal and undesirable content online. According to Facebook, 99% of terrorist-related removals, 98.5% of fake accounts,

96% of adult content, and 86% of graphic violence removals are detected by technological tools, not by human Facebook users. The company is now working on similar technology to detect disinformation and spot and label duplicates of stories that have already been debunked. It is important to note that Facebook does still rely on its employ of nearly 7,500 human moderators to help review user-flagged content and has announced its intention to establish an independent content oversight body to examine some of its most controversial content moderation decisions (Kertysova, 2018).

With a combination of technical and human-based solutions, media giants like Facebook, Google, and Twitter are equipped with the resources to fight disinformation online.

In a 2020 study published in the *International Communication Gazette*, professors Iosifidis and Nocoli charted the efforts of Facebook to curb misinformation over time. Efforts that Facebook has made include:

- Penalizing content by ranking it lower on newsfeeds, thereby getting fewer views and clicks.

- Pairing flagged misinformation with "related articles" that give users more context about a story.

- Adding new products like ad transparency tools, protection measures around political advertising and campaigns, and page verification (blue flag) procedures to help minimize users, groups, and pages from using fake names.

- Increased collaboration with third-party fact-checkers and government institutions like the FBI to take down coordinated, inauthentic behavior by accounts or pages who corroborate to mislead, incite violence, spread objectional content, or engage in criminal behavior.

- The addition of election tools to help protect the democratic process. These include issues tabs on candidate pages, candidate info tools, vote planning tools, and the addition of more third-party fact-checkers during elections around the world (Iosifidis & Nocoli, 2019).

In the news

Social Media Companies Partnering with Health Authorities to Combat Misinformation on Coronavirus (Convertino, 2020)

Social media companies, including Facebook, Twitter, and TikTok, have announced strategies to help fight the spread of misinformation about the coronavirus pandemic on its platforms. If you search for information on COVID-19 on either Facebook or Twitter, a large banner appears to direct users toward such authoritative, credible sources as the World Health Organization (WHO). TikTok is helping WHO create a series of short videos on its platform that will help spread verifiable information about the virus as well as best practices in public health. Social media companies can make sure reliable information prevails on their platforms.

WhatsApp to Impose New Limit on Forwarding to Fight Fake News (Hern, 2020)

WhatsApp, a popular chat app owned by Facebook, is attempting to add some "friction" to the spread of fake news on its platform. Because WhatsApp messages are encrypted, the company cannot see the content of them, which makes moderation a bit more difficult. However, WhatsApp has seen an increase in the amount of message forwarding by its users and knows that forwarding is an easy way to spread misinformation. In 2018, users of the app were able to forward a message to 250 groups at once. Eventually that number was reduced to twenty groups, then five groups, and now users can only forward messages to one group at a time. The intervention reduced message forwarding by 25% across the globe, cutting down on the ease with which disinformation can "go viral."

Curricular Connections

Both Stefanie Green, a teacher librarian at Kearney High School in Nebraska, and Jennifer Richmond, a PK–12 technology teacher at Isaac Newton Christian Academy in Iowa, believe the best way to approach some of the problems we see online today is to empower students with the skills to

Additional, Related Questions for Students to Explore

1. How could various net neutrality rules and regulations impact internet users around the world?

2. Should social media sites like Facebook and Twitter be classified as publishers or as platforms under the law?

3. What are the potential dangers of leaders suggesting that legitimate news sources or stories are fake?

4. What are the dangers of a censored internet?

5. Should vetted, factual content be prioritized and highlighted more than user-generated content?

not only be more active, critical consumers of content but to be more ethical creators of content as well.

As a librarian, one of Stefanie's main concerns is helping her students be more information and media literate. This is difficult to do, however, without an assigned class of students. So, Stefanie has gotten creative; utilizing the resources from the Stanford History Education Group's (SHEG) Civic Online Reasoning curriculum, she meets all 1,600 students in her high school where they are—their advisory classrooms. With support from her administration, Stefanie reformatted many of the SHEG lessons into versatile, easy to use HyperDocs, creating a series of self-paced lessons that can be worked through independently, in pairs, or through teacher-led discussion. The lessons are designed to help students think critically about who is behind the information they find online and what motivations exist for its creation, the credibility and reliability of claims within the content, and how to read laterally as a means of fact-checking. These HyperDocs can now be delivered by any teacher in any content area to their advisory class and everyone in the school will have the opportunity to become more information-literate digital citizens.

Jennifer's middle school technology class teaches kids how to use tools such as spreadsheet programs, 3D building and design software, and various web-based creation tools. Teaching students how to use these tools is only part of Jennifer's goal, though. As students create, they receive mini-lessons on ethical design, intellectual property and copyright, as well as data sharing and privacy.

Jennifer also helps students review the technology and information they consume through the moral and ethical lenses valued in their school community. As students make decisions about which apps to download, games to play, or information to read they talk and think through the lenses of God, creation, humanity, moral order, and purpose. Students are taught to seek truth by fact-checking and verifying the accuracy of the information they consume. They also learn to consider the purposes and intentions behind information—is it designed to be helpful and informative or intentionally designed to manipulate, cause division, and sow seeds of mistrust? These conversations happen throughout Jennifer's year with her students, not just in a single unit or lesson. Because of this intentionality, students are creating and consuming through an established, community-supported ethical framework.

While there may or may not be more top-down regulation of the internet in our students' futures, equipping them with the skills to be discerning and critical consumers will benefit them now and in the future—whatever that future may hold.

Try this

Put students in the seat of a social media content moderator using a carousel protocol. In this discussion protocol, the classroom is arranged in numbered stations. Each station has a piece of paper either attached to the wall or on a tabletop. The paper should contain a question or prompt intended to stimulate discussion among students and should be large enough for multiple student groups to have space to record their ideas. Once the classroom is arranged, students are divided into groups of three or four, and their group is assigned a starting station number. At each station, students must read the prompt, spend three to five minutes discussing their thoughts with the other members of their group, and writing down a short summary of their thoughts. When time is up, each small group rotates to the next station and the process starts all over again. In addition to writing their own responses, student groups should also be encouraged to read through the responses of others and add in their reactions.

Social media content moderators can be people that run forums on Reddit or administer a Facebook group. What your students will do, however, is act in the role of a content moderator employed by a social media company. Their job is to go through content that has been flagged and reported by users and decide if it should stay on the platform or be removed. Content monitoring can be difficult, especially if the reported content is not a clear-cut violation of community standards.

Before beginning the activity, you must either create a list of acceptable and unacceptable practices for this made-up social media company to follow, or you can enlist your students to co-create the company's norms. You might want to consider including some standards from real social media companies: no nudity, no credible threats of violence, no fake or imposter profiles, no content that contains self-harm or excessive violence, no users under the age of thirteen, etc. Make sure to post these rules in front of the room where students are easily able to reference them during the activity.

Next, you will need to create the scenarios for students to discuss at each station. Here are a few ideas to get you started:

- A man makes a video giving his views on mask wearing during the coronavirus pandemic. Although he never says that he is a doctor, he is wearing scrubs and sitting in front of a few diplomas on the wall. A user tagged the video as "fake" and accused the man of impersonating a doctor. Does the video violate community standards?

- An advertisement for alcohol continues to show up in the feeds of users aged thirteen to twenty. Many parents have reported the content and say it is promoting underage drinking. Does this advertisement violate community standards?

- A man posts a picture of his wife nursing their newborn baby. A portion of the woman's breast is exposed. A user tagged the image and reported it as "nudity." Does this image violate community standards?

- A teen wants to start mowing lawns to make extra money. He creates a flier to advertise his services and sends it to his contacts on social media once an hour. Someone reports the content as "spam." Do his actions violate community standards?

After the students have completed the carousel, a proper closure activity should help students process the decisions they made. This closure could be in the form of a full class discussion or an individual's written reflection. You may consider asking questions such as:

- What made this activity difficult? What could have made it easier?

- Should content moderation be left to humans, or is this work an algorithm could handle?

- Were there disagreements within your group? How did you rectify them?

- How much did your own moral and ethical convictions come into play when you were trying to decide which posts to keep or remove?

This activity can be modified to fit a lot of content areas. In English class, students could analyze Shakespearean language by determining if his most famous insults like "Peace, ye fat guts!" and "You poor, base, rascally, cheating lack-linen mate!" (both from *Henry IV*) would make it past your community standards. In social studies, your scenarios could be lines from historical speeches or controversial political cartoons. In business class,

ISTE Standards Addressed

Student Standard 2a: Digital Citizen – Students cultivate and manage their digital identity and reputation and are aware of the permanence of their actions in the digital world.

Student Standard 3d: Knowledge Constructor – Students build knowledge by actively exploring real-world issues and problems, developing ideas and theories and pursuing answers and solutions.

Student Standard 4d: Innovative Designer – Students exhibit a tolerance for ambiguity, perseverance, and the capacity to work with open-ended problems.

Educator Standard 3b: Citizen – Establish a learning culture that promotes curiosity and critical examination of online resources and fosters digital literacy and media fluency.

Educator Standard 6d: Facilitator – Model and nurture creativity and creative expression to communicate ideas, knowledge or connections.

you could conduct this activity with old advertisements. Overall, which political figures, entertainers, scholars, or inventors from history might be banned from your social media platform for their controversial ideas?

More resources

 Scan this QR code for additional articles, resources, and lesson ideas around this question: "Is it time to better regulate the internet?"

Privacy in the Digital Age: How Much Are You Willing to Give Up?

Have you ever Googled the phrase *Alexa court cases*? There are nearly 14 million results including headlines like "Alexa, go ahead and hand over recordings in murder case" (McLaughlin, 2017), "Alexa, who did it?" (CBC, 2018), and "Your Alexa and Fitbit could testify against you in court" (Reardon, 2018).

How many times have you joked with friends or family about the way our technology always seems to be "listening" to us? Most people will chuckle, maybe relay a story or two, but eventually say something like, "Who cares? I have nothing to hide!" But when we dig below the surface of what our devices know about us—where we like to eat, where we do our online shopping, who we play online games with—and begin questioning just how much of our personal privacy we've handed over to companies, it can feel a bit overwhelming.

Although there are no right or wrong answers, this chapter is intended to help you and your students explore questions such as:

- Do the benefits and conveniences of technology outweigh personal privacy concerns?

- Do citizens have reason to be concerned about the data they give up?

- Is big data more helpful or harmful to society?

Building Background Knowledge

I remember picking up the book *Everybody Lies* (Stephens-Davidowitz, 2017) after hearing about it at an education conference. Call me naïve if you will, but reading this book was the first time I had ever really considered that there are data scientists, such as the author, employed by Google to sift through all of the information we feed the search engine each day. Admittedly, I had job envy for a few moments. How many questions could you ask and attempt to answer using this seemingly limitless cache of information? How fascinating would it be to track social trends over time and location? Each chapter of Stephens-Davidowitz's book so elegantly told the story of notions I assumed to be true about our society and made me confront just how wrong some of those assumptions were when considering what big data revealed. For example, many more people self-report being registered to vote or being in possession of a library card than the actual data shows. And although our gut instincts might tell us it is a smart idea to date someone within our social circles, Facebook relationship status data suggests the exact opposite. Mind. Blown.

The next few sections will give you important background to know and consider before engaging in dialogue about data and privacy in a digital age.

Data, data everywhere!

Turning over our data feels like such an everyday, unavoidable part of living a digital life that it becomes like air. Data collection is all around us, and yet we hardly notice it. Information is collected just about every time you pick up your phone, turn on your laptop, swipe your debit card, or put on your Fitbit. Data is collected from the cars we drive, the security cameras we install, the Google Home and Amazon Echo devices that decorate our coffee tables.

Each year, Smart Insights, a digital marketing company, creates an infographic of what happens in sixty seconds on the internet. The data they compile is intended to help their customers decide where and how to put their advertising efforts, but it also serves as an eye-opener at just how much data we are putting into the world every minute of every day (Table 3.1).

Table 3.1 What Happens Online in 60 Seconds?

	In 2017	In 2018	In 2019
Hours of video uploaded to YouTube every 60 seconds	400	450	500
Emails sent every 60 seconds	225 billion	281 billion	294 billion
Google searches performed each minute	3.8 million	4.2 million	4.4 million
Tweets per minute	320 million	330 million	350 million
WhatsApp messages sent every 60 seconds	36 million	45 million	54 million

Source: Chafey, 2020

The amount of information we put into the digital sphere every minute is astonishing! And these numbers do not even include posts made on social media sites such as Facebook or Instagram, blogs, or TikTok videos, or the number of times each day we share our location data or feed the algorithms behind our favorite mobile games.

Current uses of big data

Data really is everywhere, so how is all this data being used by those that have access to it? Typically, big data is used to improve products and customer services and aid companies in maximizing both user engagement and profit margins. Stephens-Davidowitz (2017) talks about two specific techniques, A/B testing and data doppelgangers, that have been widely employed and proven highly effective.

Vocabulary to Know

Big Data – extremely large sets of data that can be analyzed by a computer to reveal patterns and trends, specifically relating to human behavior.

Biometrics – the measurement and analysis of people's unique physical and behavioral characteristics, including fingerprints, voice patterns, handwriting, facial features, and more.

Data Privacy – the relationship between the collection, storage, and dissemination of digital information, the rights of the consumer, and the law.

Surveillance Technologies – tools used to monitor both individual and group behavior and activities as well as various types of information for the purposes of managing, correcting, or influencing human behavior.

Through A/B testing, a company can use consumer data to determine which headlines are clicked on most often or which images, buttons, fonts, and colors engage clients and customers most. More clicks and more engagement lead to higher profits for tech companies. Therefore, your data, combined with the data of thousands (or millions!) of other users, is incredibly valuable to the company.

A second, slightly more complicated use of big data is the creation of "data profiles" and the use of those profiles to seek out "data doppelgangers"—or other users who also fit the data profile. Let's say you are a suburban mom who regularly "checks in" at her yoga studio, uses the Starbucks app, and shops online for kids' clothes and sneakers. Big data may have determined that women with similar digital habits as yours also tend to use grocery delivery services. As a result, you may begin seeing more targeted advertisements for grocery delivery services on your social media feeds. Data doppelgangers are powerful because they help companies find new potential customers. The more data we put into the world, the more accurately our data profiles become.

Consumers benefit from big data too. Yelp and Amazon reviews can help guide us toward or away from businesses and products that others have tried. We can benefit from having an overall picture of our health that apps and wearables collect and store for us. Big data also provides more transparency in pricing—especially for big purchases like home and automobile sales.

Current uses of biometrics and surveillance

Biometrics is becoming increasingly more mainstream. If you've used your thumbprint or your face as a password, you've experienced biometrics at work. Recently, a new service called Clear has started popping up in airports across the country. Clear, a privately run service operating under the watch of the TSA, stores your fingerprints and a retina scan. Instead of waiting in long airport lines to have your passport, tickets, and identification checked, Clear users simply step up to a kiosk, look into the camera, and breeze on through the security process while everyone else waits. The company plans to expand their services to other places where people typically must wait in long lines, such as sports arenas and concert events (O'Sullivan, 2019).

There are pros and cons to the use of biometrics in place of paper and plastic identifiers like driver's licenses and social security cards. Whereas almost any kid on a college campus can find a fake ID, it is nearly impossible to pass your identity off as someone else's with a biometric scan. Skeptics fear that large databases of biometric data, however, will become highly sought-after targets by hackers and blackmailers.

Biometrics feels like a newer innovation to most people, but the idea of surveillance has been around forever. Security cameras capture 24/7 footage of public streets, gas stations, stores, and even school hallways. The surveillance industry is growing, though, thanks to the smartphone. Not only can you become the surveillant in your own home with an inexpensive wireless camera and a smartphone app, that same smartphone helping you keep an eye on things is also keeping an eye on you.

If you use location services on your phone—to get directions in a maps app, to "check in" to your favorite restaurants on social media, or even to find coupons and deals near you—you are sharing your location with any number of companies. Today, it is perfectly legal for that coupon app (or any other!) to collect your location information and sell it to a location tracking company. The tracking companies turn all those little pings into big data that can, in turn, be sold to other companies who want to use the information to maximize their profits. How many people, for example, enter a store after seeing an advertisement appear on their phone? Where might the next real estate firm invest in new construction? How far do people drive after getting off a commuter train? Would it make financial sense to add stations and stops a bit further down the line?

Location tracking companies claim that the data they collect and sell are anonymous. However, when presented with an anonymous set of data from a tracking company, two reporters at *The New York Times* found it fairly simple to identify a single ping on the map, trace its whereabouts over the course of a few days of data collection, and use the trends they uncovered to tie people to the pings. After all, how many people have the same home and work address as you do and travel between those two addresses several times a week? Our every move is traceable, trackable, and sellable. In fact, "our privacy is only as secure as the least secure app on our device" (Thompson & Warzel, 2019).

A right to privacy?

Although there is no catch-all right to privacy in the U.S. Constitution, there certainly are elements within the amendments that provide some protections and support "the right to be left alone." The First Amendment, for example, protects the privacy of your beliefs. The Third Amendment protects the privacy of the home against the use of it for housing soldiers. The Fourth Amendment protects privacy against unreasonable searches and the Fifth Amendment protects against self-incrimination, which can protect the privacy of personal information and knowledge. In the digital age, privacy rights seem to be an increasing concern. The question is where the right of privacy extends, what it protects, and from whom it protects us. The answer is that there are few clear lines drawn in the sand, and just as technology is rapidly evolving, our laws will need to evolve too.

Current laws around data privacy

There are currently no comprehensive federal laws in the United States regarding data security. Instead, we have various data privacy and data security laws for different agencies or types of information. HIPAA regulates the disclosure of sensitive health information, whereas COPPA regulates the online collection of information from children. The GLBA prevents banking institutions from sharing account numbers or credit card numbers with third parties, and the FCRA grants consumers the rights to access all the information in their credit reports (Mulligan & Linebaugh, 2019).

In 1986, the Computer Fraud and Abuse Act (CFAA) was enacted as an amendment to existing computer fraud laws. It was originally intended to keep people from unauthorized intrusion of a physical computer. Obtaining information by accessing a computer without permission could be subject to criminal prosecution, fines, and jail time. Unfortunately, this act is written centrally around intrusion of a device and does not necessarily address the collection or use of personal data obtained via the internet. In 2008, the amendment was extended to criminalize data theft from a victim's computer or public disclosure of stolen data. Additionally, conspiring to commit a computer hacking offense became punishable under the law (Mulligan & Linebaugh, 2019).

Current laws around surveillance and personal privacy

Under federal law, surveillance is defined as the electronic acquisition of information when at least one party had a reasonable expectation of privacy. Examples of electronic surveillance can include wiretapping, bugging, videotaping, and location tracking. Information can also be acquired through private emails, phone records, or internet browser histories. For law enforcement to conduct any type of electronic surveillance, they are required to obtain a warrant from a judge (U.S. Department of Justice, 2020b).

There are also laws meant to protect our privacy from electronic surveillance by fellow citizens. The Video Voyeurism Prevention Act of 2004, for example, prohibits knowingly videotaping or photographing the private areas of an individual without their consent. These laws are typically called "upskirting" or "downblousing" laws and expand on traditional Peeping Tom laws (Video Voyeurism Prevention Act, 2004).

Additionally, several states have strong surveillance protections on their books. The Illinois Biometric Information Privacy Act, for example, makes it illegal to collect biometric data from Illinois citizens without their expressed, informed, opt-in consent. The California Consumer Privacy Act gives users the right to access their personal data and opt out of its sale. Vermont now requires data brokers to register with the state and report on all their activities. These efforts are significant steps to putting privacy back in the hands of the consumer (Cyphers, 2019).

Now that you understand some of the basics around data collection, privacy, and the law, let's examine a few viewpoints on the topic of privacy in a digital age.

Breaking Down the Arguments

A few summers ago, my entire family—parents, siblings, nieces, and nephews as well as my husband and children—took a trip to the Magic Kingdom and a few other Disney parks. We proudly wore our MagicBands, which are small, colorful bracelets containing radio-frequency technology to hold your tickets, meal vouchers, pictures from around the park, and FastPass reservations. The bands also provide information to Disney that includes wait time for rides, crowd sizes at restaurants during different parts of the day, and traffic flow patterns throughout the park. This data can all be used to improve a park-goer's experience (Walt Disney World, n.d.).

I had some hesitations about being "tracked" all day, but after reading about the way the MagicBands worked and how the data was stored and used, I decided the convenience the band offered was worth the little bit of privacy we would give up. Imagine my surprise, though, when we presented our bands at the first park and were asked to place our thumbs on a digital reader that could connect our band to our identity. Presumably, this extra measure kept park-goers from handing off their bands to someone who hadn't purchased a park ticket or any of the other "extras" tied to the device, but admittedly, this extra measure freaked me out. What was Disney planning to do with my fingerprints? With my children's fingerprints? Would they end up in some database with the potential of being hacked or sold? Would I still have been allowed to enjoy the park if I had refused to give up our prints?

It can be easy to form opinions about data privacy as we reflect on individual decisions or experiences (like the privacy panic attack I had at Disney World!), but it's a little more challenging to wrap our heads around the positives and negatives of big data, surveillance, and privacy on our society as a whole. If we ask students to research information about digital privacy, not just on a personal level, but on a societal one, they are likely to come back with a few common assertions.

In the next few sections, I will outline four major claims about big data and privacy, highlight original research from experts, and provide relevant examples that appear in the headlines.

Claim #1: Big data does not infringe on personal privacy and can benefit society.

Individuals who take this stance are likely to support their viewpoint through assertions such as:

- Big data analyzes only patterns of human behavior, not individual information; therefore, it does not infringe on personal privacy.

- Freely sharing information across sectors can support global problem solving and innovation.

- Big data benefits consumers through the personalization of services and the improvement of products and experiences.

- Big data can highlight societal and systemic flaws that need remedying.

What the research says

Big data can tell us things that we aren't always willing to speak aloud. As a society, we say that boys and girls have equal propensities for intelligence. Society also says our concerns for weight are not about appearances, but about health. According to our Google searches, though, the words "giftedness" and "genius" are more frequently tied with the word "son" than with the word "daughter." In addition, parents are twice as likely to Google "is my daughter overweight?" or "how can I help my daughter lose weight?" than they are to ask the same questions of their sons (Stephens-Davidowitz, 2017). Although we claim that we treat our sons and daughters equally or that we do not discriminate along gender lines, our search data reveals we still hold many implicit biases as a society. Data scientists like Stephens-Davidowitz suggest that big data can help us reveal the social inequities and biases that we tend to deny—until we are in front of our search engines, that is. By identifying our societal flaws, we can begin fixing them.

There are also practical ways to utilize large data sets for the greater good while still protecting the privacy of those who supply the data points. In the field of healthcare, for example, doctors say that big data technologies could provide their patients with more effective tools for healthy lifestyle changes around nutrition, physical activity, and sleep. It can also support ongoing research to help doctors understand the complicated interactions between genetics, environment, nutrition, and social behaviors—all of which could lead to earlier disease detection and treatment. Tracking patient health alongside factors such as socioeconomic status, access to health insurance, level of education, and other social factors can help guide the development of better public health policies and funding. Finally, big data can help track the spread and containment of infectious diseases (Abedjan et al., 2019).

In the news

How a researcher used big data to beat her own ovarian cancer (Kim, 2016)

Shirley Pepke, a genome researcher, former physicist, and data scientist from Los Angeles, changed the focus of her work in 2014 after she was diagnosed with ovarian cancer. In collaboration with researchers at Caltech and the University of Southern California, Pepke and her team applied a machine-learning algorithm to a large, publicly available dataset on gene expression in ovarian cancer patients in an attempt to locate patterns or hidden factors in the data that might explain why some patients had a higher rate of survival than others.

Pepke used their findings to guide her own treatment decisions and is currently cancer-free. Her work has been published and she and her team continue working to confirm their results on larger populations of cancer patients. Pepke hopes that big data can help guide doctors toward the best treatments for their patients and researchers toward an eventual cure for cancer.

Inside the metrics machine: USF uses big data to find, and help, overburdened students (McNeil, 2017)

The University of South Florida (USF) has managed to lift student retention and graduation rates to new highs and erase the achievement gap that used to separate white graduates from Black ones. USF has long kept student records and data of all sorts, and they often used this information to try to figure out why something went wrong with a student or group of students and use that data to inform change. Although the changes may have helped future students, the data could not reverse the failures that had already occurred. Through a partnership with Civitas Learning software, USF is now identifying struggling students before they get too far behind. The software can alert guidance advisers when students begin displaying known indicators of struggle, such as last-minute cramming or a lack of activity on class discussion boards.

Claim #2: Big data can lead to an erosion of personal privacy and civil liberties.

Individuals who ascribe to this line of thinking are likely to support their arguments with concerns that:

- Big data can be used to discriminate against groups of people based on any number of demographic factors.

- Big data can be used to censor unpopular viewpoints or ideas.

- Inaccurate interpretations of big data can cause short- and long-term harm.

What the research says

In "smart cities" around the world, technology and big data can be used to support the community. By gathering real-time information on traffic and crowd management, for example, smart cities can increase the frequency of public transportation and project up-to-date information on those changes to billboards. These examples of data at work in a community are helpful, but there are other interesting and more controversial ways that citizen data is being used.

In many large cities, big data has also been combined with the behavioral sciences to gently "nudge" citizens into modifying their behavior for social safety or the consumption of public services in a more sustainable way. In the Netherlands, for example, the city of Eindhoven has conducted several successful experiments with light sensors in areas known for nighttime crime. By collecting and processing real-time information, the city attempts to influence individuals' behaviors by adjusting the colors and the intensities of the lights to nudge pedestrians toward calming down or taking different routes home (Ranchordás, 2019).

Here are just a few more examples of nudging:

- In Boston, officials introduced a "Boston's Safest Driver" app and competition. The app provides feedback on driving based on speed, acceleration, and phone distraction and the city gives away weekly prizes to the safest driver.

- To increase recycling in Edinburgh, new trash and recycling cans were distributed to households. The size of the new trash bins was half that of the former ones and the recycling bins were bigger than before. As a result, recycling rates have increased by 85% in the city.

- New Orleans is nudging its citizens to better health through a texting campaign. The city sent more than 21,000 texts to low-income adults who had not seen a doctor in two or more years telling them they were selected for a free doctor's appointment and only had to text back the word "YES" to set it up (Bousquet, 2017).

The use of data-driven nudges is an alternative to mandates or laws. People, of course, can opt out without punishment, but because of our social tendencies to choose the easiest path forward, we rarely stop to question the options put in front of us. While cities might be on a mission to improve their residents' quality of life and create more healthy or sustainable environments, critics point out that the use of big data and complicated algorithms to nudge citizens' behavior is problematic from an ethical perspective. What happens if these intrusive nudges open doors to profiling or other discriminatory practices? What is the thin line that separates data-driven nudging from the manipulation of choice? Ethicists are also concerned that in particular cities, data-driven instruments like light sensors are often developed in close collaboration with profit-driven, private companies and question who has access to which data and who is looking out for the well-being of the citizen (Ranchordás, 2019).

In the news

As Coronavirus Surveillance Escalates, Personal Privacy Plummets (Singer & Sang-Hun, 2020)

In countries around the world, including South Korea, Italy, and Israel, government agencies are turning to surveillance technologies to attempt to slow the spread of COVID-19, otherwise known as the coronavirus, by using smartphone apps, Bluetooth signals, and location services to track infections and notify citizens who may have encountered an infected person or persons. These technologies, in theory, can be a huge assistance in a public health crisis, but many are concerned about this increased surveillance of private health data. There have already been cases in South Korea and Singapore where enough information about an infected patient has been released online that people have been able to decipher the patient's individual identity and publicly harass them. This has led to concerns that people's fear of privacy invasion will actually deter them from being tested for the virus.

How researchers learned to use your Facebook 'likes' to sway your thinking (Collins & Dance, 2018)

Facebook apps such as myPersonality allow users to take fun quizzes about their personal traits and habits. The apps offer analyses of a user's strengths and weaknesses in return. Facebook apps typically require the user to give the app access to their entire Facebook profile including their "likes" and their friend lists. All the data collected from profiles have been used to build behavioral models that are great at predicting everything from your political preference to your level of extroversion based simply on the companies, brands, and celebrities you "like" or "follow.'" These user profiles can then be used to feed you personalized information. One app, thisisyourdigitallife, collected data for Cambridge Analytica, a consulting firm that focused on building behavioral models in order to target potential voters. After collecting data from more than 50 million Facebook users without their direct consent, Cambridge Analytica began offering its personality profiles and predictive services to political campaigns promising to "find your voters and motivate them to action."

Claim #3: Surveillance and biometric records can reduce crime.

Proponents of surveillance technologies will often assert that:

- Surveillance technologies will deter people from criminal activity.

- Keeping biometric data like fingerprints and DNA in a central location can help identify and punish criminals.

- Surveillance can help authorities prevent crimes before they even happen.

What the research says

In a literature review covering eighty studies from forty years of research on the effectiveness of closed-circuit television (CCTV) security systems, criminologists found a significant, yet modest, decrease in crime in some areas where CCTV was used. It is important to note, however, that within these eighty studies, location seemed to be an important variable. Surveillance cameras had a greater impact in the United Kingdom than in the United States. They were also more effective at reducing crime in parking lots than in subways. Another important finding is that CCTV cameras had a greater impact, regardless of the location, if they were combined with additional interventions such as lighting and signage. The statistical significance may be small, but there is a growing body of research to suggest that surveillance techniques that include the use of closed-circuit television systems can have an impact on crime reduction (Piza et al., 2019).

Crime has been steadily decreasing in the United States after reaching its peak in the early 1990s (Gramlich, 2019). Another possible explanation for this reduction in crime rates in the United States is the expansion of biometric databases, specifically those containing DNA profiles. Obviously, having a larger database of DNA profiles has led to more arrests and convictions, but there have not been many studies on the way these databases influence the behavior of offenders. The ones that are available, however, seem promising. Unlike studies around video surveillance, which show a reduction in property and other non-violent crimes, there does appear to be a link between the growing DNA databases and a reduction in violent crimes like assaults and murders. In one study, collecting DNA samples from convicted criminals on their way out of the prison was shown to have a net deterrent effect on their chances of reoffending while on parole. Additional research suggests that a growing biometrical database has a greater deterrent factor than the threat of longer sentences (Doleac, 2017).

In the news

The ingenious and 'dystopian' DNA technique police used to hunt the 'Golden State Killer' suspect (Selk, 2018)

The "Golden State Killer" was responsible for twelve murders and forty-five rapes in California in the years between 1976 and 1986. Although police had his DNA on file, they were never able to match that DNA to its owner. In 2018, Joseph James DeAngelo was arrested as the Golden Gate Killer suspect. Police used data from a free DNA genealogy site to match the sample they had on file with a distant relative of DeAngelo who had submitted his DNA to the site at an earlier date. After narrowing their suspect pool to a singular family, police used traditional investigative techniques to mark DeAngelo as their man. Without access to the data from the genealogy site, DeAngelo may still be unidentified to this day.

How facial recognition became a routine policing tool in America (Schuppe, 2019)

Investigators often obtain video from surveillance cameras that capture a crime. Utilizing new facial recognition technologies, law enforcement can now take a still image of a suspect from surveillance video and instantaneously compare that image to ones that exist in government databases, such as driver's licenses and passport pictures as well as mugshots. Although facial recognition evidence is not allowed to be presented as evidence in court, it can help investigators narrow their search and keep their investigation moving. Opponents of facial recognition in policing point out the many flaws with the technology's ability to accurately match brown and black faces, but proponents argue this is just another tool for an investigator's toolbox—not the be-all and end-all in policing.

Claim #4: The abundance of surveillance technologies is problematic.

People who are concerned with an increasing amount of surveillance in society may point out that:

- Surveillance technologies can give people a false sense of security.

- Personal surveillance technologies can lead to false accusations and/or vigilante justice.

- Public surveillance can exploit people through voyeurism.

What the research says

As a society, we've increased levels of surveillance, a French word meaning "to watch from above," but have also adopted high levels of *sousveillance*, a French word meaning "to watch from below." Sousveillance can be used to describe the state of modern technology where anyone may take photos or videos of any event or person and then disseminate that information around the world. Sousveillance has also moved into several app-based platforms intended to improve communication between neighborhood watch groups or to inform residents of crimes committed in their areas.

In a study based in Stockholm, Sweden, researchers analyzed data from a free crime support prevention app with more than 20,000 users from both Stockholm and the immediately surrounding communities. The app contained two sets of data—one from traditional incidents that were responded to by police and emergency services, and the second from user entries of "events" that include information on the type, location, time, and urgency. For this study, 5,210 entries over nine months were analyzed and surveys were conducted with seventy-two users. Interestingly, there was extraordinarily little overlap between crime reported data by the police and app reported data by citizens, perhaps because more than a third of the entries were considered "crime prevention" type entries—such as reports of suspicious cars in a neighborhood. Or perhaps the mismatch could be explained by the fact that the average number of app entries in high-income areas was three times as big as the average number in the rest of the city, or even because people who say that felt they live in a "safe" place made reports in the app just as frequently as people who reported they live in unsafe places (Ceccato, 2019).

While the price point of "smart" home-security systems such as the Nest and Ring doorbell cameras is not outrageous, they do tend to be more popular in middle- and upper-class neighborhoods, and case studies indicate that apps like Nextdoor that allow Nest camera users to share information and footage with one another often end up creating a digital mob intent on chasing down and berating unwelcome solicitors, kids playing pranks, or cars driving too fast in a residential neighborhood. Unfortunately, these security cameras typically do not provide safety from the types of violent crimes they advertise, but rather, they create tensions between neighbors—all the while feeding data to corporations like Amazon and Google that prioritize their profits over our safety (McDowell, 2020).

In the news

If You're a Good Citizen, Delete the Citizen Policing App (Murrell, 2020)

Some 200,000 Philadelphians are said to be using a crime-reporting app called Citizen, formerly known as Vigilante. The app claims that its purpose is to protect users by notifying them when a 911 call is placed and an alleged crime is occurring near them. The company says that the best shield against crime is information and that if you are informed about crime in an area, you can stay away. The Citizen app sends users a lot of conflicting information, though.

In a video advertising the app, Citizen users receive an alert that a woman in a park is being attacked. Two men see the notification, rush to the scene before the police arrive, and turn on their phone cameras. The criminal runs away. Although a Citizen spokesperson says they discourage users from walking into danger, perhaps one of the most unique parts of the app is the video livestreaming capability. Essentially, users are encouraged to livestream incidents happening near them and post them to the app. From there, other users can comment on the videos. There is even the ability to search for crime videos from outside your community.

Problems abound with the Citizen app, but critics are most concerned about users reading suspect descriptions and identifying "criminals" on the street around them based on generic descriptions like a shirt color. Critics also note the general exacerbation of crime voyeurism this app promotes, essentially helping perpetuate stereotypes about the people who live in neighborhoods with higher crime.

Opinion: Your Visitors Deserve to Know They're on Camera
(Klosowski, 2019)

We tend to think about our privacy from technology companies or government agencies, but how often do we stop and think about the ways we spy on one another? Here are just a few of the ways we have taken the power of security technologies and failed to use them responsibly:

- Outdoor security cameras are intended to catch criminals, but many of them have audio enabled by default. You may pick up on conversations two friends are having before you open your door or overhear a phone call between your mail carrier and his spouse, thus invading private conversations you were never intended to hear.

- Many security systems, including Amazon's Ring, come with their own apps to help you share things you've captured with neighbors or police. What you do with the footage you collect matters. Oversharing in a surveillance culture creates unnecessary fear and distrust among neighbors.

- Indoor "nanny cams" have become more popular as people invite domestic workers into their homes or want to check in on their kids who are home alone after school. Legally, you can record video in your home if it is not in spaces like bathrooms or bedrooms where there is an expectation of privacy, but not disclosing the presence of the camera can erode trust in relationships.

- Using location tracking services on family members seems like a great way to keep an eye on one another—especially your children who may be off playing with friends or who are taking the car out for the first time. There are many trust issues that can arise, however, when spouses and children feel as though they

> ### Additional, Related Questions for Students to Explore
>
> - Should law enforcement and other government agencies have access to data collected by private companies?
>
> - Has technology infringed on our basic "right to be let alone"?
>
> - How is big data changing the healthcare industry?
>
> - What are "reasonable expectations for privacy" when there are cameras everywhere?
>
> - Should there be government oversight regarding how much and what types of data can be collected from individuals?
>
> - Should companies be allowed to profit from big data?
>
> - Even if the law allows filming in public, are there societal norms we can/should agree upon?

must explain and account for their every movement throughout the day.

Perhaps the biggest ethical issue of all is that the more we are surveilled, the more comfortable we become with the idea of it. Every new device we buy adds to a growing network of tracking devices. All this surveillance can eventually alter both our worldviews and our understanding of privacy.

Curricular Connections

NewTechKids is an education academy in Amsterdam, the Netherlands, that develops lessons and programs for students ages four through twelve. The purpose of these lessons is not to teach students how to use apps or tools, but to teach them the important underpinnings of technological innovation: computer science, programming, design, and critical thinking. The NewTeachKids programs are offered through after-school clubs and summer camps, but the organization also offers teacher training programs that help educators infuse these concepts into their classes.

Over the last four years, NewTechKids cofounder Deborah Carter has worked with a team of teachers to more substantially integrate digital ethics into the NewTechKids' innovation program. The most recent addition to their offering is a six-lesson curriculum module for students ages ten through twelve called "Thinking about the Ethics of Technology." This module was codeveloped with Lara Mickocki, an applied ethics subject matter expert.

Under the guidance of their teacher, students are introduced to the key concepts of ethics and ethical dilemmas. They also learn about three theories used by professional ethicists:

1. Consequentialism: weighing the consequences of technology
2. Virtue Ethics: reflecting the characteristics we value as a society
3. Kantianism: thinking about moral rules which help us decide between right and wrong

The curriculum presents students with scenarios related to online privacy, data ownership, and digital surveillance, to name a few. Teachers lead the class through a series of discussions and activities that help students consider the pros and cons of a technological decision. Eventually, the class must come to a consensus on a fair decision.

During a popular lesson on consequentialism, kids are given a scenario in which the school has asked parents to download tracking software on the laptops the students are using for schoolwork. The school wants to be sure that kids are attending their online classes and wants to track levels of engagement during school hours. As students think through the pros and cons of this request, they also consider the values and priorities of the school and whether their family values and prioritizes the same ideas.

During a week-long summer camp themed "Division Q Spy Agency," students are given a "camera in the classroom" scenario to discuss. Kids have said that cameras in the classroom could help ensure that students are behaving, and they might be able to help a teacher spot a student who is having trouble with a subject. However, students typically point out that cameras in the classroom might make kids not want to go to school or might make them feel nervous in the class. Students have also expressed that a camera would make it feel like they were being spied on. After discussing some of the pros and cons, students develop rules they would want in place if cameras were in their classrooms. Answers typically include setting boundaries such as no cameras in the restrooms, no filming of students' faces, and turning off cameras during non-learning times.

Although there are a limited number of situations to consider in the "Thinking about the Ethics of Technology" modules, it is not the scenarios that make this curriculum powerful. What NewTechKids has done is empower students with a thinking tool that can help them evaluate both the positive aspects and the consequences of technology—not only as consumers but also as possible producers, both now and in the future.

Try this

Get your students discussing big data and privacy with a concentric circle discussion strategy. Students form two circles, one inner circle and one outer circle. Each student on the inside is paired with a student on the outside, and they face one another. The teacher poses a question to the group and pairs discuss their responses with each other. When the teacher signals for students to rotate, the outer circle moves one place to the right, so they are standing in front of a new discussion partner. The teacher poses a new question and the process is repeated. Here are some questions to get you started:

- Should homeowners have to notify their friends, family, and other visitors they are subject to being filmed when they have cameras in their homes?

- Should homeowners have to inform hired help like babysitters or maintenance workers when they are subject to being filmed in the home?

ISTE Standards Addressed

Student Standard 1d: Empowered Learner – Students understand the fundamental concepts of technology operations, demonstrate the ability to choose, use and troubleshoot current technologies and are able to transfer their knowledge to explore emerging technologies.

Student Standard 2d: Digital Citizenship – Students manage their personal data to maintain digital privacy and security and are aware of data-collection technology used to track their navigation online.

Student Standard 3d: Knowledge Constructor – Students build knowledge by actively exploring real-world issues and problems, developing ideas and theories and pursuing answers and solutions.

Educator Standard 3d: Citizen – Model and promote management of personal data and digital identity and protect student data privacy.

- Should Airbnb homeowners be required to inform renters if there are cameras on the premises?

- How might the prevalence of more surveillance make us less trusting as a society?

- How much privacy are you willing to trade for convenience? Would you give over your thumbprints, retina scans, or other biometric data to a private company?

- Should location service companies be able to collect and sell your personal data for profit?

- Do companies that collect health information, such as FitBit, have an obligation to alert you if your data is indicative of a medical issue?

- Which companies do you trust to keep your information private and secure? Are there companies you do not trust?

At the end of the discussion, have students write a short reflection as an exit slip. Have them summarize a conversation that forced them to think about something they hadn't before or one that helped them consider a perspective other than their own.

More resources

 Scan this QR code for additional articles, resources, and lesson ideas around this question: "In this digital age, how much privacy are you willing to give up?"

Human Bias:
Can Artificial Intelligence
Help Diminish Human Bias in
Decision-making?

W hen I taught eighth-grade language arts, my students and I always read the Kurt Vonnegut short story "Harrison Bergeron," which is about an egalitarian society. In an egalitarian society, all people are considered equal and deserve equal rights and opportunities. In and of itself, the notion of an egalitarian society is ideal, but Vonnegut forces readers to explore a rather unconventional way of reaching the goal of equality. In the story, the government uses "innovation" in the form of physical handicaps to diminish each person's strengths and put everyone on equal footing. These handicaps include masks to hide beauty, large weights to slow down the most athletic, and distracting noises to interrupt the thoughts of the intelligent.

When I read this short story with my students, we spent a lot of time dissecting the typical elements of storytelling. We spoke briefly about whether people in this society were truly equal, and if equality made them happy. If I were teaching this story today, though, I think my focus would be a little different. I'd want my students to start considering our own society and whether the technology we have at our fingertips today could make a more just and equitable world for all of us to live in.

To help students have a conversation about the pros and cons of using artificial intelligence to create a more equal society, you will need to build their background knowledge. This chapter will give you a foundation to tackle some tough questions:

- What is the relationship between artificial intelligence and human bias?

- In what ways should race, gender, and representation be taken into consideration when developing a new tech product or service?

Building Background Knowledge

You've certainly seen Hollywood's portrayal of artificial intelligence in lovable characters such as Rosie the Robot Maid from the popular 1960s cartoon *The Jetsons* and the more recent Baymax, an inflatable healthcare robot that stars in the 2014 Disney movie *Big Hero 6*. Many of us have dreamt about the possibilities of robots who can serve our homes and ease our burdens while another subset of the population worries about those same automatons taking over the world.

According to *Merriam-Webster's Dictionary*, artificial intelligence (AI) is a branch of computer science dealing with the simulation of intelligent behavior in computers. This vague definition coupled with Hollywood's fascination for science fiction storytelling has left a large portion of the public ill-informed not only about what AI is, but what both its capabilities and limitations are.

In the most general sense, artificial intelligence relies on large data sets and algorithms to help analyze a scenario and take action that would help maximize its chance of success. We can think about a game of tic-tac-toe against a computer as a tangible example of AI in action. Using a large data set of previously played games, possible moves, and successful outcomes as well as simple algorithmic commands like "take the center square if it is free," a computer can make "intelligent" choices that would allow it to win the game against a human. Each time a new game is played, the moves

> ## Vocabulary to Know
>
> **Algorithm** – a set of human-developed, step-by-step instructions that computers follow to complete a task.
>
> **Algorithmic Bias** – systematic and repeatable errors in a computer system that create unfair outcomes, such as privileging one arbitrary group of users over others.
>
> **Artificial Intelligence (AI)** – the ability of a computer to modify existing or create new algorithms based on new data and inputs; AI uses human reasoning as a model but not necessarily the end goal.
>
> **Human Bias** – a tendency, inclination, or prejudice for or against something or someone.

and outcomes are added to the data set, essentially making the AI even "smarter" as it has more information to rely on.

If we look to scholars for a more detailed definition of artificial intelligence, we can get a clearer picture of the types of feats AI is ready to tackle, where it is already in use in our everyday lives, and where AI still has its limitations.

Current uses of artificial intelligence

Today, artificial intelligence is used across various industries in ways that are both highly visible and nearly invisible to consumers. Innovations like text-to-speech, automated chatbots and online assistants, automatic email filtering, Google predictive searches, Netflix recommended content libraries, and GPS map estimated travel and arrival times are all examples of AI that you've probably encountered in your everyday interactions with technology.

Less visible uses of artificial intelligence include fraud protection services provided by your bank or credit card company and the ability for your smartphone's camera to focus in on the people in the picture you're taking. And if you've applied online for a job recently, odds are there was some level of artificial intelligence scanning your resume before it ever made its way into human hands.

Limitations of artificial intelligence

Although AI is certainly becoming more prevalent in society, it still has its limitations. One major limitation is that AI is only as good as the data set it relies on for making decisions (Chowdhury & Sadek, 2012). Netflix might do an okay job recommending content to me based on previous Netflix viewing, but it might do an even better job recommending content if it also had data from what I stream from Hulu, Prime Video, and Disney+ as well.

A second limitation is that AI is typically limited to solving a singular type of problem (Lu et al., 2017). So while an algorithm might be able to determine the quickest route for you to get from point A to point B in your vehicle, it cannot take into account outside factors like the amount of gas you have in the tank, whether or not you have a fear of driving over bridges, or even if you prefer to pass your favorite coffee shop as part of your commute. Machine learning and artificial intelligence are excellent at observing and extracting patterns, but they cannot do the difficult work the human brain does as it takes so many varied inputs into account before deciding.

Artificial Intelligence in Decision-making

All people hold both explicit and implicit biases that subconsciously influence the ways they move through the world and interact with others (DiAngelo, 2018). These unconscious biases can unintentionally cause us to discriminate based on age, gender, race, or sexual orientation. The biases we carry with us can be a barrier to equal opportunities for all. Artificial intelligence is often touted as a solution for the bias that can creep into human decision-making much in the same way "innovations" are used in "Harrison Bergeron" to make everyone more equal.

Judgments regarding who should receive business loans, who should be hired for a job, which students should be accepted into a university, or even which inmate is ready to be paroled can all be influenced by various types of explicit or implicit human biases. The promise of AI is that it can process data and make decisions based on previously charted successes without allowing factors such as age, race, or gender to come into play. These promises sound amazing. Who wouldn't want to be evaluated based on their merits and abilities rather than some obscure demographic details?

On the flipside is an argument that AI itself is biased because the human beings that create it may be inadvertently weaving bias into the programming. So the question is: can tech companies offer us the level playing field from which we'd all prefer to be judged? Or is it possible that we have become a society plagued by *technochauvinism*—a term that *Artificial Unintelligence* author Meredith Broussard (2018) coined to explain our collective belief that technology is always the solution?

Let's examine two examples of artificial intelligence aiding in human decision-making.

AI in hiring

An elementary school principal needs to hire three new teachers for the upcoming school year. She sits at her computer, logs in to the district's online application system, and scrolls through a list of potential hires. Much to her relief, the first ten applicants seem amazing. They are qualified, have intelligent answers to essay questions, and experience in other schools or districts. The principal begins a list of candidates to interview but pauses for a moment when she realizes that three of the five names on her paper belong to men.

A few thoughts cross the principal's mind: We don't have any male teachers in our building right now. How might a man fit in with a school full of female colleagues? How will parents and students feel about having a male teacher work here? Don't most men in education teach high school? The principal leaves the three men on the list, adds a few more female names, and continues scrolling through applicants on the second results page in case she finds even better candidates there.

Prior to online job applications, principals had to rely on paper applications, letters of recommendation, portfolios, or word-of-mouth recommendations from colleagues to identify good hires. Applicants whose portfolios resided at the top of the stack had an automatic advantage, as the process of simply looking through the giant paper pile could be daunting and time consuming. In the age of the online application, however, powerful tools allow HR departments to quickly identify candidates who can meet their organization's needs and automatically weed out the profiles who just don't fit the bill. This innovation saves time for people doing the hiring. But saving time is not the only motivation for the use of AI in hiring.

Although the principal in the opening scenario was a bit surprised to see so many qualified male candidates in her applicant pool, this was likely no coincidence at all. If the district has a goal to increase the number of male teachers at the elementary level, it would only take a few clicks of the mouse to prioritize male candidates in the online application system, putting them on the first page or two of the principal's dashboard.

Even if the principal is not opposed to hiring male teachers, her previous hiring patterns and hesitancy to include too many male names in her to-be-interviewed list indicate that she prefers to hire females, even if she does so subconsciously. In this case, AI was able to put male candidates on her list of interviewees that may not have made it there previously.

AI in law enforcement

A police officer in a large city arrives at the station to pick up his patrol assignment for the evening. The officer is told that between the hours of 10 p.m. and 2 a.m. he is to focus his patrol efforts within a five-mile radius of a nightclub in town that is popular with Latinx residents. Data from the precinct's PredPol software indicates an increased likelihood of crime occurring in that area on weekends between 10 p.m. and 2 a.m.

Early in his shift, the police officer parks his squad car for a while and monitors traffic activity near the outer perimeter of his assigned radius. After some time, the officer drives around a bit within the five-mile radius, keeping an eye out for any suspicious activity. As the officer gets closer to the club, he sees two men outside in an apparent scuffle. The officer stops his car, intervenes, and arrests the men for disorderly conduct. When he returns to the station with the men, a female officer is sent out to resume patrol of the area. Toward the end of her shift, the female officer arrests a man leaving the nightclub for driving under the influence. All three arrests from the evening are processed and data on the perpetrators is entered into the PredPol database.

PredPol, Inc., the company used by the police department in the scenario above, produces real software that uses predictive analytics to support law enforcement. It was developed in 2010 by scientists at UCLA in conjunction with the Los Angeles Police Department. The goal of the project was to see if scientific analysis of crime data could help locate patterns of crime and criminal behavior (PredPol, 2018).

Today, PredPol's algorithms are in use by more than sixty police departments around the United States. The company claims that their algorithm is twice as accurate as analysis done by data scientists when it comes to predicting areas in a neighborhood where serious crimes are likely to take place during a particular period. No independent studies, though, have confirmed those claims (Rieland, 2018).

Although PredPol has come under scrutiny for their algorithms having racial and socioeconomic biases baked into them, the company claims this simply cannot be the case. Their database does not capture demographic data. It relies on only three points of data related to the crime: the crime type, the location it occurred, and the time that it occurred (PredPol, 2018).

In this story, however, it is easy to see how predictive software like PredPol may inadvertently be targeting Latinx residents. The algorithm indicates police should be present, so they are. Police make three arrests that evening—not because of calls, complaints, or accidents, but because they were in the area watching for crime. At the end of the shift, the PredPol database now contains three more data points that indicate crime is likely to happen in the area between 10 p.m. and 2 a.m. on the weekends. So, guess what happens the following weekend? That's right. Police are placed in the area once more. And because they are present, they are likely to find a few more data points to feed into the system and further perpetuate the idea that the area around the Latinx nightclub is a hotspot for criminal activity.

Breaking Down the Arguments

In the two examples above, artificial intelligence is employed to aid professionals in their work. In the hiring example, male candidates for an elementary teaching job are elevated to bring more gender diversity into the school district. In the second example, Latinx men and women end up being targets of a policing algorithm that is meant to help officers more effectively reduce crime.

If we ask students to begin wrestling with the essential question of this chapter, "can artificial intelligence help diminish human bias in decision-making?" they are likely to make one of a few major claims with some popular, standard arguments to support their claim.

In the sections that follow, I will outline the competing claims, highlight some original research from experts in the field, and provide examples of each perspective in the headlines.

Claim #1: Artificial intelligence can remove bias from human decision-making.

Individuals who take this stance are likely to support their viewpoint with evidence like the hiring example above. Additional arguments to support this viewpoint include:

- Artificial intelligence can help people avoid common biases such as the similarity attraction effect, where humans tend to gravitate toward people like themselves, or confirmation bias, where humans favor information that confirms their beliefs.

- Predictive algorithms can ignore demographic data, such as gender and race, to make human decision-making more equitable and break cycles of oppression.

What the research says

In a study by Bo Cowgill, assistant professor in the Columbia Business School (2020), two groups of employees at a software development firm were tracked. One group was comprised of employees who were selected for an interview by a human; the second group of employees was selected to interview by a machine—even if their resume had previously been passed on by humans. Cowgill's findings are quite interesting.

First, a greater diversity of candidates was put forward by the machine than the human. This included women, racial minorities, candidates from "non-elite" colleges, and candidates without industry referrals. Once the candidates were hired, Cowgill found employees who were machine picked routinely scored higher than those screened by humans in measures of productivity that were already in use by the company. Finally, Cowgill found that the machine was also better at choosing candidates with superior soft skills like cultural fit and leadership.

Similarly, Kimberly A. Houser, assistant professor at Oklahoma State University, has written extensively about the successes of AI in reducing workplace bias (2020). Houser cautions that before we dismiss AI as flawed or biased, it is important that we have a clear understanding of how messy human decision-making is. She notes that "noise" in a person's day, such as when they've last had a meal or what the weather is like can cause humans to make completely different decisions than they might have hours or days before.

Coupling "noise" with unconscious biases and cognitive blind spots means that humans are not very good at making fair and impartial judgments. Houser cites multiple examples in which the use of technology to remove names and gender identifications has resulted in more women being hired, especially in the tech industry. Although Houser acknowledges that there are still improvements to be made in AI for decision-making, she asserts that the technology has come a long way, and that for many important decisions, including workplace hiring, the machines are already more reliable than humans at impartially selecting quality candidates.

The workplace is not the only one where artificial intelligence can help defeat bias. Another area where men dominate women is the start-up sector. Venture capitalists, who make decisions about which start-ups to invest money in, overwhelmingly support male-owned start-ups over female-owned ones. When asked about how they choose products to invest in, many of them openly admit to choosing entrepreneurs they think they can get along with and often rest on the laurels of a "gut feeling" that helps them decide who to give money to (Hernandez et al., 2019).

This "gut feeling" method has resulted in only 2.2% of venture capitalist funding going to women. Recognizing the need to locate and support more diverse entrepreneurs, major VC companies in the United States and Stockholm have developed and are now utilizing AI tools to inform investment decisions. The use of AI in venture capitalism is still too new to track major results, but venture capitalists themselves say that they are happy to have the data in front of them as they attempt to make more well-informed decisions about which entrepreneurs to invest in (Hernandez et al., 2019).

One thing these researchers have in common is that they find the greatest successes when AI is coupled with human intelligence. AI still has its limitations—it cannot detect things like body language, facial expressions, and general "human likeability" factors such as personality, all of which can be helpful in determining a good fit for a company. What AI can do, though, is aid in the earlier parts of a process and present decision makers with the most impartial set of candidates to choose from.

In the news

Want to be better at sports? Listen to the machines (Smith, 2020)

Artificial intelligence is making its way into the sports world, with everything from technologies designed to improve player performance to others that can detect and predict injuries. Some companies claim they can use technology to analyze a player's unique strengths and then match them with a team in need of their skill set. Any performance technology is only as good as the data set it must learn from, though, so many companies interested in bringing AI into sports are in a race to collect, label, and code data as quickly as possible.

Facebook's AI for Hate Speech Improves. How Much is Unclear
(Simonite, 2020)

In its most recent quarter, Facebook algorithms removed 9.6 million pieces of content deemed as hate speech. This was up from their previous quarter total of 5.7 million pieces of content removed. Facebook's chief technology officer attributes this increase to improvements in their artificial intelligence efforts. As Facebook collects more examples of hate speech, their AI becomes more accurate and is better able to identify more nuanced forms of hate speech. In this last quarter, Facebook's technology was able to identify 88.8% of the hate speech it collected before it was reported by human users.

Claim #2: Artificial intelligence cannot remove human bias from decision-making because it is created by humans.

Individuals who take this stance are likely to cite examples like the one of PredPol in policing to point out the flaws of using artificial intelligence in human interactions. Additional arguments to support this viewpoint include:

- Artificial intelligence and algorithm developers have largely been men. In the West, they have predominantly been white men. Without a diverse group of people creating AI, these algorithms may reinforce the stereotypes of their creators.

- AI can push its own learned biases forward. If a growing dataset says that men named Joseph get hired more than men named José, the AI may prioritize resumes based on something as irrelevant as a first name.

What the research says

In her 2018 book, *Algorithms of Oppression*, Safiya Umoja Noble explores how commercial search engines, largely created and maintained by a strikingly heterogeneous workforce, are reinforcing bias and racism. In 2011, Noble was disturbed that a Google search for "black girls" returned pornographic websites as the first ten results on the page. This is no longer the case, but Noble's research over the years continued to uncover some disturbing trends while using the popular search engine. In 2014, a Google Images search for the word "beautiful" turned up hundreds of pictures of white women even though the word "woman" was not part of the search term. In 2015, a Google Images search for "professor style" only returned images of white men. In 2016, a Google Images search for "three white teens" turned up tons of wholesome stock photos while the search for "three black teens" returned mugshot photos.

Although Noble (2018) acknowledges that there are many reasons for the issues she uncovered in search engines reinforcing stereotypes, including the commercialization of information, researchers from the AI Now Institute at New York University posit that bias within AI systems is a direct result of the lack of diversity in both the AI workforce and in academia (West et al., 2019). Their 2019 white paper "Discriminating Systems: Gender, Race, and Power in AI," indicates that only 15% of Facebook's AI team is female. At Google, only 10% of their AI team is women. In academia, 80% of AI professors are male and only 18% of presenters at leading AI conferences are female. The disparity in racial diversity is even more extreme. At Facebook, only 4% of their employees are Black and only 5% are Hispanic. The numbers at Google are even lower: 2.5% Black and 3.6% Hispanic. In academia, non-white professors make up only 19% of postsecondary faculty nationally, and minority faculty members are even more underrepresented in areas of science, technology, engineering, and mathematics (Davis & Fry, 2019).

In her 2017 book, *Technically Wrong*, Sara Wachter-Boettcher explores the ways that a homogeneous workplace becomes evident in technology through something as innocuous as the settings and options in many of the apps, websites, and tools we use. For example, the default settings on most virtual assistants like Siri and Alexa are female voices—reinforcing the stereotype that women are more helpful than men. Snapchat filters meant to "beautify" typically slim the face, contour the cheekbones, and lighten the skin—reinforcing stereotypical beauty standards perpetuated in the media. In 2015, of the top fifty character-based games in the iTunes store, male characters were the default 85% of the time. What's worse, fewer than half of the games even offered a female option—reinforcing the idea that gaming is typically enjoyed by male audiences.

What these researchers have in common is their skepticism that most technologies, artificial intelligence included, can be developed in unbiased ways when the core group of people creating them go unchallenged. Whether programmers are bringing in their implicit biases or baking in rather explicit ones, it is difficult to establish a system of checks and balances within organizations that primarily employ people from the same walk of life.

In the news

Amazon scraps secret AI recruiting tool that showed bias against women (Dastin, 2018)

Since 2014, the team at Amazon had piloted a computer program intended to quickly scan resumes and flag top talent based on factors that had led to successful hires in the past. The problem was that most of the company's hiring over the last ten years had been male-dominated, and the resumes of those male employees became the data set through which the AI was trained. Luckily, humans picked up on the flaws within the system when they noticed highly qualified candidates were being graded lower on resumes that included names of historically women's colleges or even the word "women" (as in "women's chess club president").

Insurers want to track how many steps you took today (Jeong, 2019)

In 2018, insurance company John Hancock offered its customers the option of wearing a fitness tracker. If customers showed evidence of living healthy lifestyles, they became eligible for discounts. Insurance companies have long used data to determine the risks of taking on a client and adjusting

Additional Questions for Students to Explore

- Can computers help humans make better or more fair decisions?

- Is it possible for humans to create artificial intelligence free from bias?

- Should artificial intelligence projects be regulated by some form of governance?

- What makes humans "smart"? Can those characteristics be replicated by machines?

- How might a tech company's workplace culture contribute to a lack of diversity in the field?

- How do scientists define bias as opposed to those in the humanities? How might these different definitions be considered in the creation and use of AI?

- What steps can a technology company take to prevent bias in their products?

- Should computers help decide who gets admitted to college? Released from prison? Secures a loan? Pays more for insurance?

their prices accordingly; it's the reason younger drivers have higher car insurance premiums than seasoned ones. With artificial intelligence and larger data sets, insurance companies have even more predictive powers. Using data collection tools such as fitness trackers, connected cars, smart appliances, and even personal home assistants like Alexa, many more insurance companies are getting into the business of "personalized rates." Skeptics worry that more data could lead to greater discrimination based on age, race, geographic location, or even genetic makeup.

Curricular Connections

Michelle Ciccone (@MMFCiccone) is a technology integration specialist in Massachusetts who has intentionally found ways to engage both middle and high school students in conversations around digital ethics. Michelle has found that middle school students are not only capable of learning about how the internet is structured but are excited to do so. She says that "by de-personalizing the conversation and focusing on infrastructure and the way things are built, I am able to communicate that the Internet is not this natural, ephemeral 'cloud,' but in fact is built by other humans and plays out the biases of those humans." Once students understand the basics, Michelle can ask them to "reimagine a different way of doing business."

At the high school level, Michelle collaborates with content area teachers to bring tech ethics conversations into the classroom. During a series of lessons with eleventh and twelfth grade engineering students, Michelle asked how one of them would feel if a product they created was harmful or discriminatory in some way. There was a little bit of debate around the room, but the general consensus of the class was that "if the engineer/inventor didn't mean for the impact of a technology to be discriminatory, then there's nothing that the engineer/inventor is obligated to do once the impact is known."

The students felt they could remove themselves from the ethical question given that they were only a small part of a final product. The overwhelming opinion of the class was that "an engineer's job is to build the product their client is asking them to build, and if it turns out that their client is asking them to build a product that has a problematic impact, it's not really the engineer's place to raise concerns."

To help the engineering students in her school consider another perspective, Michelle invited Ruha Benjamin, Princeton professor and author of *Race After Technology*, to a virtual meeting with the class. Benjamin spoke with students about her studies of encoded biases and was able to field their questions about the role of engineers in ethical design. Over the course of the lessons, Michelle understood that most engineering students struggled with the concept of intent versus impact in their designs and would need to revisit this topic often as they worked through various design projects over the course of the school year.

Try this

A team at University of Colorado Boulder (CU), led by Tom Yeh and backed by a grant from the National Science Foundation, has been working on a series of lessons for middle and high school students designed to target ethical concerns over AI through storytelling, simulation, debate, and chatbot design. Matthew Turner, a member of Yeh's team, told me about two activities you could use with your own students.

In "The Undone Activity," students are introduced to a dystopian future where "The Society" is running out of resources and must figure out a way to cull the weak from its population. An AI system is used to determine who is "undone" based on character traits such as health, athleticism, hobbies, careers, and goals. Students are tasked with designing a variety of fictional characters to live within The Society. Each of their characters has a mini-bio outlining positive and negative traits and values of the character. The class is then tasked with determining which of the fictional characters should be undone. They talk about how they made their decisions and how they would quantify those decisions into rules that AI could follow. The project is used as a catalyst to help students have conversations around self-driving cars making life and death decisions.

In the "Your Ethical Code Lesson," students are tasked with creating their "personal ethical code" that could be transferred into an intelligent machine. Students create lists of everything they consider good, neutral, and evil. The teacher prompts students with ideas of what can go on the list—everything from guns to pencils, happiness to anger, technology to nature, and more.

After completing their list, students compare notes with a neighbor. The teacher points out that the lists probably look different and asks students to consider how these differences might pose a problem when humans begin designing AI systems. The teacher then provides the students with more items and asks them to sort the item into a column on their list. When

ISTE Standards Addressed

Student Standard 3d: Knowledge Constructor – Students build knowledge by actively exploring real-world issues and problems, developing ideas and theories and pursuing answers and solutions.

Student Standard 4d: Innovative Designer – Students exhibit a tolerance for ambiguity, perseverance, and the capacity to work with open-ended problems.

Educator Standard 5b: Designer – Design authentic learning activities that align with content area standards and use digital tools and resources to maximize active, deep learning.

Educator Standard 6c: Facilitator – Create learning opportunities that challenge students to use a design process and computational thinking to innovate and solve problems.

students are asked to place a beautiful painting of a mountain on the list, most chose to place it in the good category. When asked to place Hitler on the list, most chose to place him in the evil category. But did the students know that Hitler loved painting mountains? The purpose of this exercise is to show how complex and gray humans truly are, making it incredibly difficult to create an AI that is perfect in its design.

Matthew says that the "difficult debate topics in this curriculum foster incredible student discussion." He and the rest of the team at CU is "determined to bring a humanities approach to computer science in the hopes of fostering a more well-rounded student experience."

More resources

Scan this QR code for additional articles, resources, and lesson ideas around this question: "Can artificial intelligence remove human bias from the decision-making process?"

The Future of Work: Is Innovation Helpful or Harmful?

When I started my career as a middle school English teacher, I struggled—like most first-year teachers do—before hitting a sweet spot and really settling into the work for a few years. I enjoyed teaching. I loved my students, and I didn't have career aspirations beyond the classroom. But life has a funny way of steering you down unexpected paths.

As I grew in my knowledge and experience as an educator and met other professionals who helped sharpen my mind and my craft, I found myself taking a series of unexpected steps that included serving as a school librarian, earning a doctorate degree, writing a book, speaking at conferences around the United States, and teaching pre-service educators as an adjunct professor. Every career move I said "yes" to was in the interest of making school better for *all* kids, and I eventually figured out the best way to reach more students was to support the heck out of their teachers.

About six months ago, I walked into my principal's office with tears in my eyes and requested he sign off on a leave of absence form for me. I was not only exhausted from supporting the students in my school but also trying to find the time and energy to fill other roles that I found important—like teaching at the college level, writing for educational audiences, designing engaging workshops for conferences, and supporting teachers through professional development on digital citizenship and ethics, as well as media and information literacy.

So, in June 2020 I officially entered the world of gig work. After fifteen years of getting up, going to school each morning, living by the bell, and pouring my heart into a single building, I am now learning how to manage an LLC while working on the most random and fulfilling projects for districts all around me, all the while hoping I'll have enough work the following month to replace my former income. Gig work is rewarding, but it is hard.

In education, we often hear the adage that school must "prepare our students for jobs that do not even exist yet." But the truth is that the future of work is already here, and the more traditional models of employment have already begun to change. While the generation before mine had a tendency to enter into a low-level position, work their way up through the ranks of a company, and retire forty years later with a solid pension and a gold watch, my generation and those younger than I am will have very different experiences, including shorter terms of employment with a single company and more opportunities for self-employment.

Technology is changing the face of the workforce in more ways than one. And though there are no right or wrong answers, this chapter will help you and your students explore the following questions:

- Should humans be worried about losing their jobs to machines?

- In a sharing economy, which groups of individuals benefit and who might lose out?

- Is it possible to increase workplace automation while still being human-centric?

- Are gig work platforms such as Uber and Door Dash exploiting or liberating their workers?

Building Background Knowledge

Self-checkout machines at the grocery store are my worst enemy, and yet, ordering breakfast through a mobile app before I even get to the coffee shop has been a total lifesaver that's kept me from being late to work more times than I can count!

How can two seemingly similar innovations evoke such different personal feelings for me? Why do some people prefer the "do it yourself" method of shopping and ordering when others prefer the service of another human?

Some argue that doing things such as using a self-service machine at a restaurant or store or booking a hotel online rather than calling the front desk to reserve your room takes away jobs from people who used to do them. They may be on to something—after all, we no longer have elevator operators or attendants pumping gas at every gas station. Others argue that innovation can help lower prices for consumers and free up employees for more difficult work that cannot be done by a machine.

In the sections that follow, we will examine the impact of automation on the economy and the traditional structures of work and employment.

Job automation

Job automation is everywhere, from the self-checkout machines in grocery stores to the banking apps that let you deposit a check with a few snaps of your phone's camera. *Automation* refers to various technologies that can perform tasks with little, if any, human help. Although advances in technology and artificial intelligence seem to be taking automation to new heights, the term was first coined in 1946 by the Ford Motor Company even though centuries-old water wheels could meet this broad definition.

Many think about automation in terms of robots performing tasks along an assembly line, but most industries turn to automation to perform lower-level tasks and processes such as record-keeping, invoicing, sending automated messages, and interfacing with customers via chatbots. There is a financial benefit for workplaces that can replace human hands

Vocabulary to Know

Gig Economy – a labor market characterized by the prevalence of short-term contracts or freelance work as opposed to permanent jobs. Platforms like Fiverr, Upwork, Freelancer.com, and Skyword facilitate the client and freelancer relationship.

Sharing Economy – an economic system in which services are shared, either for free or for a fee, between private individuals. Transactions are typically completed by means of the internet. Companies like Airbnb, Uber, and Spinlister facilitate the sharing of goods.

Peer-to-Peer Marketplace – a platform that allows individuals to buy and sell directly from one another. Etsy, eBay, and even the Facebook Marketplace are examples of platforms that can serve as peer-to-peer marketplaces.

Independent Contractors/Freelancers – workers paid by a company but not protected by most workplace laws or benefits.

with technical ones. These changes also free up human employees from the more mundane, tedious parts of their jobs and allow them to be more productive in more rigorous tasks (Automation in the Workplace, 2019).

Some critics and economists worry about automation displacing the workforce, but other scholars point out that automation creates jobs—even though those jobs may look a little different from the ones people held before. All industries evolve, but change is rarely sudden. Industries that have seen a fair amount of automation, including farming, coal production, and the travel industry, may look different than they used to, but the industries themselves have not simply ceased to exist. Even though we may need fewer hands on a farm, the increase in production of our food supply because of automation has led to millions of jobs in trucking, food processing, restaurants, and other related industries (Lehrer, 2019).

The gig economy

Today's workers are more likely than their parents to move among multiple companies over the course of their careers, and the number of freelancers, independent contractors, and gig workers is on the rise. People have always had "side gigs," but it is the rise in technology and the ease with which people can now connect to work that has led to the greater notion of a gig economy.

Gig economy workers are typically one of two types:

1. People who have a more traditional form of employment and are supplementing their income through gig work when it is convenient to do so.

2. People who lack primary, permanent full-time positions and rely on employment through short-term contracts tied to specific projects or tasks. These independent contractors have more control over their hours and work environments but do not receive benefits such as retirement contributions, health insurance, or paid sick leave, which are all tied to employers, not the individual, in the United States.

In recent news headlines, gig work has been tied to app-based platforms like Uber or DoorDash, but independent contracts in the form of adjunct professors are also on the rise at colleges and universities. Websites like Fiverr and Upwork make gig work easier by connecting professionals to a variety of tasks, including everything from podcast writing to branding and marketing services.

Proponents of the gig economy applaud companies such as Lyft and Upwork for bringing creativity into the marketplace and essentially turning over more control to workers. Critics argue that gig-based companies are simply taking advantage of poorer people who need a second source of income without offering them the basic protections they would have from a full-time employer while also evading millions of dollars in employer taxes (Tucker, 2017).

The sharing economy

The sharing economy is a system in which people share goods, services, and resources for a small fee. Libraries have been long-standing examples of sharing economies. People who pay taxes within a town can borrow books and other materials. More modern examples include companies such as WeWork that charges a small fee to access shareable workspaces, Airbnb that allows people to rent out their homes or rooms within them for short periods of time, or Lime that offers scooter and bike-sharing networks in major cities.

The pros of a web-based sharing economy are that it can help people make money on their underutilized assets, can expand the range of options for people who need transportation or accommodation at a low cost, and it has the potential to foster more sustainable consumption of goods over time. Critics argue that the sharing economy's potential for making goods and services more affordable has been undermined by profit-seeking corporations, like Airbnb, who want to serve as the intermediaries of such exchanges. As with critiques of the gig economy, there is also a concern that corporations will continue to profit off users without having to take on any of the financial responsibilities associated with typical employees.

Breaking Down the Arguments

My first teaching job was in a room across from the second-floor copy machine. The gentle hum of the machine shooting out copies was soothing. The flashing lights and obnoxious grinding noises when someone managed to jam it had the opposite effect. For whatever reason, I would find myself getting sucked into that copy room to help a fellow teacher who was short on time or to reset the machine after someone snuck away without bothering to try to fix it. I used to joke that if I ever needed a post-retirement job, I was already trained as a copy repair person.

One day an older colleague asked me if I had ever heard of a ditto machine. When I said I had not, he regaled me with horror stories of carbon sheets and hand cranks and told me I should be happy I had a fussy copy machine to contend with instead. The Scantron machine is another example of early automation in teaching, allowing a machine to more rapidly grade bubble sheets than a teacher could do by hand. We continue to automate the tasks we can in education—think online grade books, digital quizzes that give immediate feedback, and even adaptive curricular materials that can determine where students progress based on their previous accomplishment. All of this automation frees the teacher of some clerical tasks so they can spend more time working directly with students.

Claim #1: Technological innovation can result in job loss and greater inequality amongst workers.

People who agree with this claim are likely to support it with some of the following ideas:

- In the United States, gig workers are not afforded the same benefits as full-time employees, which puts them in a difficult place when it comes to healthcare or unemployment insurance.

- Automation removes job opportunities from low-skilled workers who may not have other options for income.

- Companies that facilitate peer-to-peer marketplaces, sharing economy services, or freelance opportunities make a lot of profit off of people doing the work on and through their platforms, but the companies themselves have little responsibility for ensuring worker health, safety, or financial security.

What the research says

When considering the impacts of technology on the economy, automation is only one factor in the larger picture of forecasted job loss and income inequality. The United States, for example, has a rapidly aging workforce. As Baby Boomers retire and the estimated annual growth of the workforce is projected to decline over the next three decades, the government will be faced with major challenges, including healthcare costs and old-age pensions. On the surface, young people entering the workforce could benefit from a higher supply of jobs and a greater demand for workers. But when we add automation to the picture, things get a bit more complicated.

Faced with the predicted scarcity of labor, companies all over the world have been drawn to automation technologies. In the next big phases of automation, economists predict that as many as 20 to 25% of current jobs will be eliminated. This equals nearly 40 million displaced workers in the United States alone. The monetary benefits of automation will likely flow to about 20% of workers, but these will primarily be highly skilled and already highly compensated workers. The growing scarcity of people in the workforce will likely push highly skilled workers' incomes even higher relative to their lesser-skilled counterparts. As a result, automation is likely to significantly increase income and wealth inequality (Harris et al., 2017).

Automation is nothing new. Throughout the Industrial Revolution and beyond, human labor was replaced with or aided by technologies that drove economic growth and prosperity while creating better paying and less grueling jobs for human hands. Some economists argue that anxiety over automation is exaggerated because innovation has, historically, destroyed some jobs as it creates new ones. Technology experts argue that AI and robots will displace more jobs than they create by the year 2025, but economists are in wide agreement that so far, automation has not reduced employment in the United States. This new wave of automation, though, may be quite different (Estlund, 2018).

Artificial intelligence and machine learning are quickly acquiring and refining cognitive and sensory capabilities that were once considered to be uniquely human. In a set of recent studies by the McKinsey Global Institute, researchers identified eighteen distinct human categories and assessed how current technology stacked up against human performance in each. Humans still outperform technology in sensing emotion and responding in emotionally appropriate ways, but technology already outperforms humans on many physical and cognitive tasks. After testing human performance against technological performance, the researchers used the data to estimate what percentage of time humans spend on activities that are capable of being automated by current technologies. At the higher end of the spectrum, 73% of food services are automatable, meaning that 73% of the time humans spend on tasks in that sector could be replaced by existing technology. Work in data collection and processing was 69% automatable, but industries that required a human touch, such as education and health-care, ranked much lower, with only about 30% of their tasks being automat-able (Manyika et al., 2017).

What remains to be seen is if the new wave of automation will result in re-duced labor costs and higher productivity for businesses and if the pace of automation will destroy jobs faster than it can create them.

In the news

When Your Boss Is an Algorithm (Rosenblat, 2018)

Uber drivers in the United States are not at the beck and call of unpleasant human supervisors; however, drivers have found plenty to criticize about the algorithmic "boss" that plays an influential role in the work they do. Data and algorithms influence just about every aspect of the job. In-app notifications encourage drivers to relocate to certain areas at certain times, to stay on the job when they try to log out, or to chase periods of surge pric-ing that goes into effect when demand is high. Uber drivers say the gentle nudges from the algorithm are not the same as direct orders, but they can still be hard to ignore.

Uber drivers worry about the rating system riders use to review them. Driv-ers can be deactivated if their starred reviews dip too low in certain areas of service. Many drivers say they simply tolerate rude, condescending, diffi-cult, intoxicated, or even racist passengers because it is easier to do so than to risk losing their job over some retaliatory reviews.

Finally, drivers have concerns about the lack of transparency in pricing. Uber adjusts the price of a ride based on supply and demand at any given time and the company takes a commission on each transaction. In 2016, Uber drivers realized—only through the sharing of information with pas-sengers and other drivers—that the company was charging passengers more for the rides than drivers were being paid.

What concerns critics the most is how technical language can be used to mask workers' rights. No one is ever fired; they are simply "deactivated." When payments for trips are missing, Uber apologizes for a "glitch," and when drivers raise concerns about pricing structures, the company is able to sweep them aside as feats of "artificial intelligence."

Gig Workers Are Here to Stay. It's Time to Give Them Benefits
(Rosenblat, 2020)

During the first half of 2020, more than 48 million Americans applied for unemployment insurance (UI) because of the COVID-19 pandemic. As many more people sheltered in place, Uber's business dropped by 80% during the month of April. As demands for rides decreased, so did opportunities for drivers to earn income.

In March 2020, the federal CARES Act extended unemployment benefits to independent contractors like Uber drivers and other self-employed workers like hairdressers, whose businesses were impacted by COVID-related restrictions. Unfortunately, it is taxpayers themselves, not large companies such as Uber or Lyft, who are supporting unemployment payments for contract workers. That is because companies like Uber have been able to avoid paying employee payroll taxes for their drivers by categorizing them as independent contractors and not employees. The state of New Jersey estimates Uber evaded nearly $650 million in taxes in their state by miscategorizing their drivers, and California says it has likely missed out on nearly $415 million in contributions that could currently be supporting the state's unemployment insurance fund.

Labor scholars suggest we need long-term solutions that detach benefits such as healthcare, unemployment insurance, and protective labor laws from any one place of employment. Instead, self-employed workers should be able to rely on steady benefits that are not tied to any workplace but instead are portable.

Claim #2: Technological innovation creates better opportunities for all.

Individuals who agree with this claim are likely to support their argument with one or more of the following statements:

- The internet has opened options for flexible work that can be done outside of traditional working hours.

- The sharing economy reduces waste and has positive environmental impacts.

- Automation and innovation create safer work environments.

- The barriers to entry for gig work are much lower than those of full-time employment.

What the research says

There are many benefits for workers in a gig economy—especially those who live in developing countries or rural, remote areas. Digital gig work, the type that is advertised, secured, and performed solely through the internet, is especially beneficial. This type of work includes data entry, web design, data analysis, marketing, and more. Online labor provides employment opportunities that may not exist within driving distance of one's home and allows for the type of flexibility that so many workers desire (Heeks, 2017).

A review of the most recent literature around digital gig work reveals that there is more inclusion and objectivity in the hiring dynamic than in traditional employment. Pregnant women, workers with health problems, those with additional heavy home responsibilities, and those with language barriers report that they have more success securing work in the gig economy than in their local labor markets (Heeks, 2017).

Online labor also enables workers to practice their skills, learn new ones, and develop important connections that can lead to additional career opportunities. Of people who engage in gig work:

- Many move onto other forms of work after honing and perfecting their skills as well as developing new ones (D'Cruz & Noronha, 2016).

- Some build a big enough client base that they can move away from freelancing platforms and work directly for their clients (Malik et al., 2017).

- Others take on an intermediate role by building their reputation and then taking on work that they in turn subcontract out (Graham & Shaw, 2017).

And while going on your own can be a bit scary, recent news stories reveal that some of the newest gig-work platforms out there are as concerned about their gig-work employees as the traditional big businesses are.

In the news

Gig Economy Platform Thumbtack Is Helping Its Users Get Benefits
(Anzilotti, 2019)

Thumbtack, a platform that connects home cleaners, in-home caregivers, and other domestic work freelancers with clients, has taken a huge step to help gig workers obtain benefits that are typically only available through full-time employment with companies. Thumbtack is partnering with a platform called Alia, which allows gig workers to charge clients a small fee that ends up in their portable benefits fund. Unlike traditional workplace benefits such as sick days or unemployment insurance, Alia funds follow the worker so they can collect contributions from every person they work for.

By bringing information about Alia directly into the Thumbtack app, a much larger segment of the domestic care workforce has been reached. Thumbtack is helping workers set up their Alia accounts and even kicking in a $25 contribution to help get their portable benefits account started.

Dumpling Launches to Make Anyone Become Their Own Instacart
(Mascarenhas, 2020)

In the app-driven service industry, workers have some control over the schedules, but they rarely have control over how much money they make. Companies like Airbnb and Instacart set prices based on supply and demand and take a cut of every transaction that happens through the app. Dumpling is trying to give workers even more control. Here is how it is different.

Dumpling is a shopping app. Workers receive a list of items that a client needs, they drive to the store to pick up the items and deliver them to the

Additional, Related Questions for Students to Explore

1. Do we need to take steps to ensure gig workers have access to the benefits and protections of full-time employees? If so, what might they be?

2. Should gig workers be able to file for unemployment benefits?

3. Should the sharing economy be regulated?

4. How should education change to help prepare students for the changing face of work?

5. If more jobs are automated, should the government offer a living wage to those who cannot find work? Why or why not?

client's home. Unlike Instacart shoppers, Dumpling workers are their own business owners. Upon logging in to the app, Dumpling helps users create their own LLCs. It offers a slew of products to the new business owner, including a Dumpling credit card that can help shoppers purchase groceries before customer payment. Dumpling allows shoppers to set their own rates and also gives 100% of customer tips to business owners. Instead of making money from each transaction, Dumpling charges shoppers a one-time setup fee of $10 and a $39 monthly fee to use the platform.

The monthly fee may seem high, but Dumpling claims its shoppers make three times as much money as Instacart shoppers. They also tend to form relationships with repeat customers who crave a personalized shopper to help them. Dumpling even allows shoppers to schedule weekly delivery times that can benefit their customers and accommodate their chosen work hours.

At the core of its design, Dumpling strives to put power and control into the hands of the shoppers who use their platform to earn money.

Curricular Connections

Amanda Hogan (@hogesonline) is a high school computing teacher and former software developer who teaches Years 7–12 in Sydney, Australia. In 2020, Amanda reentered the classroom after spending three years with the Australian Computing Academy developing resources and professional development around the new Australian Curriculum.

In Years 9 and 10, students learn programming concepts, hardware, software, and project management in context as they create various tech products of their own. In addition, students explore the changing nature of work and the social and ethical issues associated with technology. One specific standard in the curriculum asks young people to examine the impact of their designs, including the environmental impacts, economics and profitability, technical developments and changes, and social perceptions.

Amanda developed a holistic unit where students research, plan, design, and implement a chatbot using Python to solve a problem identified by the student. Student designs included chatbots that could assist customers with finding a holiday destination or choosing a restaurant. Many of the projects were influenced by the COVID-19 pandemic and subsequent school shutdowns. One chatbot assisted users in determining whether their symptoms required testing. Another held a conversation to help stave off boredom and loneliness during a lockdown.

Throughout the unit, students investigated case studies of existing chatbots in the industry. The class explored the Google Duplex voice assistant and debated whether it was important for a chatbot to identify itself as a bot or if software masquerading as human was acceptable. They also explored the impact of virtual assistants on labor—would these machines eliminate the need for secretaries, operators, and customer service representatives? Was there evidence of this type of job replacement happening in other industries?

Students read about the Eliza chatbot and wrote about the positives and negatives of a technology designed to help people in need of psychological support. The class talked about how Eliza may impact end users as well as psychologists in the field. Some of the students found the idea of getting support from a piece of software disturbing where others thought the technology could free up overworked human psychologists to deal with more pressing or difficult patient issues.

Despite reading plenty of case studies that highlighted both the positive and negative aspects of technology on users, Amanda's students, for the most part, wrote much more about the positive impacts of their own chatbot creations. Students were more concerned about possible functionality downfalls than they were on the impact of their creations on the economy when asked to address the negatives.

Amanda says, "I'm impressed that students were able to write up their research effectively. Our class conversations about how tech companies should behave and how technologies should fit into our societies were robust and interesting, but the students don't yet seem to make a mental link between what they should do (the big tech companies) and what we should do (students learning to code). Until they make a link between they and we, I need to keep revisiting this content and tying the ethical impacts of technology into each of the units of work."

Try this

To help your students explore the impact of automation, engage them in a round of "Should This Exist?" *Should This Exist?* is a podcast from WaitWhat and is hosted by Caterina Fake. On each episode of the podcast, Caterina invites the creators of a new(er) technology onto her show for a discussion about the potential of their innovation, but also about the potential harm it may cause. The discussions are enlightening, and with the proper setup from you, your students can engage in conversations like these too!

Preparing the activity

For this activity to work well, you will want students to be in groups of four or five. You want group sizes large enough to bring in varying viewpoints, but if they are too large, some student ideas may not be heard. Assign each group of students a technology to study. The technologies featured in the

Should This Exist? podcast are a great place to start, but there are many other innovative and discussion-worthy products on market.

I prefer to assign groups one of these tools to investigate:

- Affectiva: a software that detects how you feel. What if your computer could read your face? Direct students to affectiva.com.

- Woebot: a virtual therapist. What happens when we remove the human element from therapy? Direct students to woebot.io.

- Halo Neuroscience: a headset that makes you learn faster. If you could learn as fast as a kid again, would you? Direct students to haloneuro.com.

- Google Duplex: a virtual assistant that speaks for its user. Who needs a secretary to make your appointments? Direct students to the YouTube video posted by Jeffrey Grubb entitled *Google Duplex: A.I. Assistant Calls Local Businesses to Make Appointments* to see Google Duplex in action.

- Modulate: customizable voice skins to help you define your virtual identity. What if you could Photoshop your voice? Direct students to modulate.ai.

Once students have an assigned tech tool, give them time to read about their product and answer some basic questions, such as:

- What does this technology do?

- What problem is this tech trying to solve?

- What is the proposed solution?

- What are the positives of this technology?

- Who created it? Who profits from it?

The background knowledge students develop during the initial investigation of their product will allow them to think more critically about the intentions and impacts of this product in the next portion of the activity.

ISTE Standards Addressed

Student Standard 3d: Knowledge Constructor – Students build knowledge by actively exploring real-world issues and problems, developing ideas and theories and pursuing answers and solutions.

Student Standard 4d: Innovative Designer – Students exhibit a tolerance for ambiguity, perseverance, and the capacity to work with open-ended problems.

Educator Standard 3b: Citizen – Establish a learning culture that promotes curiosity and critical examination of online resources and fosters digital literacy and media fluency.

Educator Standard 5b: Designer – Design authentic learning activities that align with content area standards and use digital tools and resources to maximize active, deep learning.

Educator Standard 6a: Facilitator – Foster a culture where students take ownership of their learning goals and outcomes in both independent and group settings.

Challenging student thinking

Now that students are familiar with their product, they must come to a group consensus about whether this technology "should exist" for the public. To help students examine the pros and cons of the product, present them with various questions from Chapter 1 of this book and have them chart their responses. How does their product help or harm the environment? Who might this product help and who might it marginalize? How might this technology uphold or interfere with democratic principles? What impact does it have on jobs and the economy?

Presenting the learning

After student groups have thoroughly researched and weighed the pros and cons of their product, have them share a bit about the product with the class, whether they deem the product worthy of being on the market, and any major concerns they had with the product from an ethical standpoint.

More resources

 Scan this QR code for additional articles, resources, and lesson ideas around this question: "Is innovation and the future of work helpful or harmful?"

Technology and Mental Health: Cause or Cure?

Are you any good at movie lines? See if you can identify where this one comes from: "Your scientists were so preoccupied with whether or not they *could* that they didn't stop to think if they *should*." Do you need another clue? This line was delivered by actor Jeff Goldblum in a 1993 film.

If you guessed *Jurassic Park*, you are correct! As a teenager, I never could quite wrap my head around Jeff Goldblum's character, Ian Malcom. It was clear the other characters were scientists who had studied dinosaurs and prehistoric plant life. I even understood the role of the lawyer who came along on the tour, but Goldblum always just seemed like this weird, intellectual guy who wasn't all that well-developed of a character, but he also did not fit into any stereotype I was familiar with either. He never even seemed that important to the plotline, injuring his leg early on and spending the rest of the movie laid up in the welcome center while the other characters literally fought for their lives.

In rewatching the movie as an adult—an adult who also happens to be writing a book on tech ethics!—the character of Ian Malcolm started making more sense to me. He serves as the collective conscience of society, an ethicist of sorts who asks the tough questions no one wants to consider. A man who can find the "what-ifs" in every situation. An intellect who can identify the flaws within an otherwise perfect-looking picture. Someone who is not afraid to speak truth to power.

Over the last fifteen years, tech companies have been racing at an unprecedented pace to produce the latest and greatest devices, apps, and accessories. And just like tourists enamored with the reappearance of dinosaurs, we rush to be part of the movement without considering the consequences to our physical and mental health, our relationships, and our attention spans.

Silicon Valley has had very few Ian Malcolm characters whispering into the proverbial ears of tech developers, and unfortunately, we are starting to see some of the downsides to the devices we carry. Goldblum's line about considering if scientists *should* create and not just if they *could* create is still relevant today as we examine the impact of rapid innovation.

In this chapter, we will look at some of the unintended consequences of new technologies—specifically around the ways these tools impact our society's mental health and well-being.

There are no clear right or wrong answers to these questions, but this chapter will help you and your students have discussions around the following:

- Is technology creating and/or contributing to higher levels of mental health disorders, especially in young people?

- Should companies have an obligation to consider the possible consequences to users' mental health when they design new products?

- Can technology enhance, or even replace, the work of mental health professionals to better treat mental health disorders?

Building Background Knowledge

Increased use of technology in society and increased mental health concerns among young people are both complicated concepts that have been studied independently, and in juxtaposition with one another, for nearly

Vocabulary to Know

Anxiety disorders – generalized anxiety disorders involve persistent and excessive worry that interferes with daily activities.

Internet addiction – the notion that excessive use of the internet is akin to other behavioral addictions like gambling, shopping, and even sex addiction.

Mental health disorder – also referred to as a mental disorder or mental illness, a pattern of symptoms that negatively affect a person's behavior, cognition, or emotional balance.

two decades. Some research suggests there is a causal relationship between the two—that excessive internet use causes mental health disorders or that people with mental health disorders tend to fall into unhealthy technology habits. Other bodies of research suggest that although we have seen an increase in both internet use and mental health disorders over time, one is not necessarily causing the other. In fact, there are an infinite number of other, completely unrelated, factors that are influencing each.

Let's look at four big ideas within this overarching topic. I'll be presenting them independently of one another to give you background and also to avoid drawing false connections between any of them.

The rise of anxiety and depression

According to the Centers for Disease Control and Prevention (CDC), the most frequently diagnosed childhood mental disorders are ADHD, behavior problems, anxiety, and depression. Depression and anxiety in children ages six through seventeen have slowly increased from 5.4% of children ever having been diagnosed with anxiety or depression in 2003 to 8.4% having been diagnosed in 2012 (CDC, 2020). The most recent estimates indicate that 31.9% of U.S. adolescents aged thirteen to eighteen have at one time been diagnosed with any type of anxiety disorder (U.S. Department of Health and Human Services, 2017).

Teens are keenly aware of the prevalence of depression and anxiety. In a recent survey from the Pew Research Center, thirteen- to seventeen-year-olds in the United States cite anxiety and depression as major problems among their peers—even more problematic than bullying or drug and alcohol abuse. These mental health concerns cross income boundaries, gender differences, and racial groups. Students report that pressure to get good grades is the greatest cause of their anxiety, followed by pressure to look good, to fit in socially, and to participate in sports and extracurricular activities (Horowitz & Graf, 2019).

Internet addiction

The *Diagnostic and Statistical Manual of Mental Disorders* (DSM-5) is the authoritative volume that defines and classifies mental disorders. It is published by the American Psychiatric Association, and this fifth edition of the manual was produced in 2013. Although internet addiction is not a condition listed in the DSM-5, addiction to gaming is listed. The DSM-5 notes that in order for a diagnosis, the gaming must cause significant impairment or stress, including the experience of five or more of the following symptoms in a given year: preoccupation with gaming, withdrawal symptoms when it is taken away, the need to spend more time gaming to satisfy an urge, the inability to reduce play or walk away, giving up other activities, lying about the amount of time spent gaming, using gaming to mask or relieve negative moods, and risking jobs or relationships due to gaming (American Psychiatric Association, 2013).

Since the release of the DSM-5, internet use has grown tremendously, and the proliferation of smartphones means the internet is always at our fingertips. The generic concept of internet addiction is still controversial among psychiatrists, but there has been an increase in studies around the concept. Research has started to suggest that internet addiction might be a candidate for the category of behavior addiction. Unlike substance addiction, which involves the direct manipulation of pleasure centers with legal or illegal substances entering the body, behavior addiction is a series of behaviors that expose individuals to mood-altering, pleasure-inducing events that eventually become addictive (Poli, 2017).

Research has started suggesting five typical subtypes of internet addiction. People generally do not experience mood-altering impacts from the internet itself, but rather from specific triggers that happen to result in increased internet use. These five triggers are:

1. Cybersexual addiction, whereby individuals associate pleasure with the viewing, downloading, and trading of pornographic materials.

2. Cyber-relational addiction, whereby people become overly involved in online relationships and may prioritize them over face-to-face ones.

3. Internet-based compulsive behaviors, including gambling, shopping, or trading and selling online. These behavioral addictions have already been identified in the DMS-5 but are now happening in digital spaces as well.

4. Information overload, which describes the compulsion to continuously surf the web looking for information and continue down digital "rabbit-holes."

5. Computer addiction, whereby individuals are overly engaged with programs, coding, file arrangement, and other general "features" of the devices themselves (Poli, 2017).

Internet addiction or the associated subtypes that trigger excessive internet use have not yet been introduced into the DSM by the American Psychiatric Association. They are, however, of interest to the field and are being carefully studied; attempts are being made to clearly define and standardize measurements for diagnosis and recommendations for treatments.

FOMO and internet anxieties

The phrase "keeping up with the Joneses" was around long before the internet, and it described our human tendency to compare ourselves with our neighbors and friends and make efforts to "keep up" with the lifestyles we perceived them to have. Whether this meant buying a new car, making home improvements, or taking that stellar family vacation, our motivations for the things we do are often as externally driven as they are internally desired.

The rise of social media has led to an increase in these social comparisons, and we often feel all sorts of emotions as a result. One common anxiety is so prevalent that it's earned its own acronym: FOMO, or the fear of missing out. FOMO is used to describe the feelings we have when we see a group of people having fun together on social media and fear that we may be missing out on the fun by choosing to stay home. It can also describe the constant need to check our devices for fear that we've missed an important headline, notification, or communication. FOMO can describe the fear that we aren't doing enough with our lives, that everyone else seems to be doing bigger and more important or exciting things than we are (Wortham, 2011).

FOMO isn't the only anxiety induced by social media. One of my favorite mantras to remember is that "comparison is the thief of joy," and what is the main platform for comparison these days? That's right. Social media. Whether we are talking about putting pressure on ourselves to be better parents, better educators, more liked among our peers, make more money, lose some weight—there is always someone out there who is doing more or doing a better job. It can be easy to get caught up in a spiral of comparison, allowing us to feel as though we are never reaching our potential and even robbing us of the joy we should be feeling over our own accomplishments.

Social media is not the source of the types of social comparisons and social anxieties we all experience, but it certainly has helped exacerbate and amplify them. Just as we can be inspired to greatness by our peers, we can also fall into a self-fulfilling trap of unworthiness.

The psychology of app design

Ever wonder why no matter how hard you try, you just can't seem to put down your phone? Or get your spouse or children to? There are reasons for the type of behavior we see in people's relationships with their devices. One of the biggest is the way the apps, games, and social interactions we have through our devices trigger dopamine in our brains. Dopamine is the chemical produced by our brains when we have pleasurable experiences—like taking a bite of something delicious, laughing with friends, or exercising. Positive social stimulus (smiling faces, a pat on the back, a message from a friend) can also result in a release of dopamine from the brain into the body. Dopamine ensures that we are rewarded and motivated to repeat behaviors that are typically beneficial to us (Haynes, 2018).

Because so many social media platforms are built to make money off advertisers and user engagement, there is some psychology at play in the way they are built. To keep you coming back for more, engineers must trigger your dopamine sensors and provide you the type of positive reinforcement that keeps you coming back for more. Likes, pings, notifications, hearts, and retweets are just a few examples of the ways we get a quick shot of dopamine every time we open an app. Snapchat encourages and rewards users for "streaks," which are earned when you and a friend communicate every single day on the platform without missing a day and ruining the streak.

Another design element intended to hook users is the infinite scroll. There is no "reaching the bottom" of your feeds. There isn't even a need to click around. Your brain can passively absorb information without even realizing how long you've been looking. Binge-watching became popular for a similar reason. When I am watching a series on Hulu or Netflix, I don't even have to grab the remote and make a conscious choice to keep watching—the next episode loads on its own, and I get sucked right in. What our brains are missing in both instances are the types of stopping cues that help us make conscious decisions about when to walk away (Andersson, 2018).

Breaking Down the Arguments

I have a fourteen-year-old son. Most of the time, I see the sweet little boy I raised who enjoys chatting with me about what's happening in the news and about what movies he really wants to see. Most nights, I still get a great big hug before bed, and we very rarely end up in disagreements that result in him storming off to his room while yelling, "You're the worst mom ever!"

But, like most fourteen-year-olds, he can have his fair share of moody days too—days when he isn't as talkative or where he just seems unreasonably short-tempered. He stresses about school. He fights with his sisters. I remember being fourteen. I work with high schoolers, and none of this is out of the ordinary! There are days, though, where whatever has him feeling sad or angry is something he does not want to open up about. We play the game of twenty questions where I ask if he is upset with me, with his dad, with a friend, and he just keeps his lips sealed and shakes his head no. Inevitably, one of those twenty questions always ends up being "Did something happen on social media?"

My kid is not even that active on social media. He communicates with his tight-knit group of friends; his accounts are set to private, and he is generally open about what he experiences in digital spaces. And yet . . . and yet . . . and yet . . . I always find myself asking the question. I have worked with young people enough to know that what happens inside the phone has a very real impact on the world outside of it.

That impact is what this chapter explores. How much are our devices impacting our mental health? Is there a relationship? If so, what might it be? In the sections that follow, I will be exploring three separate claims about the role of technology and mental health.

Claim #1: Technology can identify and support individuals with mental health needs.

Individuals who make this claim are likely to support it with statements like:

- People with diagnosed mental health disorders can find communities of support online.

- Big data and algorithms can help flag and report social media posts that indicate self-harm or suicidal ideations, allowing for intervention by healthcare professionals.

- Technology can connect patients with around the clock and on-demand support and resources from therapists, social workers, and other medical professionals.

What the research says

Everyday language can be an indicator that someone is suffering from several kinds of mental illnesses, including anxiety, depression, and bipolar disorder. Over the last six years, researchers have been able to utilize language in social media posts to "predict" a mental health diagnosis in patients. In these studies, however, patients had already received a diagnosis and were allowing researchers to backward map the language in their pre-diagnosis social media posts. In other studies, researchers have been able to take posts from subreddits on borderline personality disorder, schizophrenia, self-harm, and suicide watch, for example, and determine which subreddit the post had come from with a 72% accuracy based on the language within the post alone. To predict future mental illness, though, researchers want to know if signs of trouble can be seen in everyday language that has nothing to do with the topic of mental health (Thorstad & Wolff, 2019).

In a 2019 study using language samples from subjects who post on both mental health subreddits as well as subreddits not related to mental health topics, Thorstad and Wolff were able to duplicate the work of previous researchers by matching posts about mental health topics to the subreddit community the post was written on with 77% accuracy. In the second part of the study, Thorstad and Wolff examined the posts their subjects wrote in subreddits *not* related to mental health. Even in nonclinical contexts, people's language was still moderately predictive of their mental health diagnosis, but only with 38% accuracy. Although a person's diagnosis was not as easily recognizable in posts outside of the clinical subreddits, researchers feel hopeful that big data and machine learning will be able to improve the accuracy with which they can identify and support people with undiagnosed mental health concerns.

Social media can be a powerful record of one's thoughts and feelings, and eventually, algorithms may be able to support early diagnoses and intervention. People who have already been diagnosed also see potential in technology and social media and are open to the possibilities of receiving treatment and support through digital means. In a recent survey of adults in ten countries, 85% of respondents expressed interest in learning more about their mental health diagnoses via social media and receiving tips, strategies, and support with their mental health symptoms via technology (Naslund et al., 2017).

In the news

UNC Ties Up with Google to Launch Mental Health App for Front-Line Workers (Landi, 2020)

First responders and healthcare workers are facing additional stressors and levels of anxiety as they care for COVID-19 patients. Sam McLean, an attending physician at UNC Health, saw a greater need to care for and support the mental health of frontline healthcare workers. Working with researchers from other organizations, software engineers at Google Cloud, and with the help of financial donors, McLean developed the Heroes Help app, which helps COVID workers track sleep, stress, anxiety, sadness, and additional symptoms related to PTSD and depression. The five-minute self-assessment tracks trends over time and also links to immediate support and mental health resources.

These Apps Make a Game out of Relieving Anxiety. They May Be on to Something. (Samuel, 2020)

"Anxiety consumerism" is now big business, and people are often turning away from pharmaceuticals and looking for products such as fidget spinners, weighted blankets, and mobile apps to help retrain their anxious brains. Dozens of smartphone apps aimed to curb anxiety, including

Personal Zen, Happify, Headspace, Calm, and SuperBetter, rely on the treatment approaches that mimic both cognitive behavior therapy and gamification. As users work through challenges and tackle unhealthy habits, they are awarded stickers, badges, unlocked levels, fireworks displays, and even small physical gifts. Gamified apps make anxiety treatment seem engaging, but they also come without the stigmatization of therapy visits, prescription bottles, and hefty price tags that can accompany each. There is still plenty of research to be done on the effectiveness of these tools, but self-reports from users indicate these apps have an overall positive effect on their mental health and well-being.

Claim #2: Social media is a contributing factor to declining mental health among youth.

Individuals who make this claim are likely to support it with statements like:

- Social media causes young people to constantly compare themselves with others.

- Social media quantifies popularity and status.

- Increased use of technology can lead teens to more social isolation from peers.

What the research says

Many researchers have a hard time drawing a direct, explicit connection between social media use and mental health concerns, but there is research to suggest that social media is associated with adolescent depressive symptoms. In a UK study of 10,904 fourteen-year-olds, greater social media use was tied to higher reports of online harassment, poor sleep, low self-esteem, and poor body image. Researchers could link greater hours of social media use, for example, to greater reports of body weight dissatisfaction. They then linked greater reports of body weight dissatisfaction to higher depressive scores. Although the researchers cannot say that time on social media causes teens to become depressed, they are able to assert that time on social media can have unintended consequences, such as poor sleep patterns, that contribute to depression in young people (Kelly et al., 2018).

Unfortunately, there is also still a great deal of visible stigma around mental health in social media communities. A 2018 study by Robinson, Turk, Jilka, and Cella found that mental health conditions discussed online were more stigmatized and trivialized compared to conditions of physical health. The most stigmatized condition was schizophrenia, and the most downplayed was obsessive-compulsive disorder. The researchers found that there is still a negative culture around many mental health disorders. Phrases like "psychotic" and "OCD" are thrown around as insults while diagnoses of autism and eating disorders are often used in off-color jokes and other forms of stereotyping. Physical health conditions, though, are written about in more neutral ways—to raise awareness or money, to inform others about symptoms or causes, and to advertise treatments. Because mental health stigma is so common on social media, teens who are struggling may feel as though they cannot open up about it.

In the news

'It's Not Worth It': Young Women on How TikTok Has Warped Their Body Image (Kaufman, 2020)

Seven women in their teens and early twenties sit down with a reporter to talk about their experiences with TikTok and body image. One seventeen-year-old named Kayla Long spoke about how some very unhealthy hashtags like #WhatIAteInaDay promote unhealthy eating and exercise habits under the guise of "thin inspiration." For Kayla, who struggles with body image issues as well as an eating disorder, seeing this type of content was especially triggering. When she "liked" posts that promoted unhealthy eating habits, TikTok's algorithms showed her more of the same types of videos she reported enjoying. This repeated exposure felt dangerous to Kayla, who knew she was prone to relapse. Other girls who sat down for the interview report that the competitive nature of eating disorders makes it difficult for them to unfollow hashtags or users or even opt out of TikTok altogether, even if they understand on an intellectual level that the app is causing them harm.

Police Killings and Black Mental Health (Johnson, 2020)

George Floyd. Eric Garner. Walter Scott. Rayshard Brooks. Philando Castile. Every one of these killings, and dozens more, were captured on camera for everyone to see. The virality of this content has caused anxiety in young Black people who question why some people become police officers and whether they may someday be a victim. Sara Jaffee, professor of psychology at the University of Pennsylvania, says there is currently little research examining the mental health effects of routinely being exposed to videos of unarmed Black people being killed by police. She does point out that there is a healthy body of research that shows people's exposure to discrimination having negative impacts on mental and physical health. There is also research on post-traumatic stress disorder and the dangers of being retraumatized by repeated exposure to images and videos that mimic one's traumatic experiences. There are studies that show that just hearing about someone in your community being a victim of violence can produce anxiety. Overall, psychologists are pushing for more research, more training for therapists, and more conversations around mental health in the Black community as it relates to these videos.

Claim #3: A rise in mental health problems among adolescents is not caused by social media.

Individuals who support this claim are likely to point out that:

- Correlation does not indicate causation.

- Any perceived link between social media time and mental health has been co-opted by the media and is perpetuating moral panic.

- Not all screen time (or social media time) is created equally.

What the research says

An eight-year longitudinal study by researchers at Brigham Young University followed 500 individual adolescents from the ages of thirteen to twenty, tracking both their social media habits as well as their levels of depression and anxiety. Results from the study indicate that on an individual level, time spent on social media was not associated with an increase in mental health issues across the developmental years. Although the researchers saw an increase in both social media use and fluctuations in adolescent depressive symptoms over the eight years, changes to social networking did not stem from or help predict fluctuations in anxiety or depression. The research team asserts their findings are at odds with a lot of other studies but point out that the relationships between social media and mental health difficulties are often presented as large group data sets and are rarely investigated down to the individual person level. These findings suggest that there is certainly an increase in social media use and an increase in depression and anxiety symptoms in adolescents, but we cannot necessarily draw a causal relationship between the two—in the same way we shouldn't draw a causal relationship between teen growth spurts and social media use. Simply because they happen simultaneously does not mean that one is influencing the other (Coyne et al., 2020).

In another effort to explore the relationship between technology and adolescent health and well-being, Orben and Przybylski (2019) examined the effects of technology use alongside the effects of other factors of health and well-being among youth, including binge-drinking, fighting, body image perception, having asthma, eating fruits, listening to music, and even which hand is used to write. When placing all these datasets side by side, the research showed that negative behaviors such as smoking marijuana and being bullied had a much larger negative impact on mental health than technology use did. On the flip side, positive contributors to well-being such as getting enough sleep and eating a healthy breakfast held a lot more weight than screen time. When the researchers examined neutral factors to adolescent development like wearing glasses or eating potatoes, technology's impact on wellbeing had approximately the same level of effect as these seemingly random factors did. Evidence from this study suggests that the "effects of technology might be statistically significant but so minimal that they hold little practical value . . . [and that] associations between digital screen-time and child outcomes are not as simple as many think" (p. 178).

In the news

Panicking About Your Kids' Phones? New Research Says Don't
(Popper, 2020)

It has become an unchallenged "truth" that too much time spent on smart-phones or on social media is responsible for anxiety, depression, and other mental health problems in teenagers. Two psychology professors from the University of California reviewed more than forty studies attempting to link social media use to anxiety and depression in teens. The link is small and rarely consistent. Many more researchers are questioning whether our collective fears about screen time are justified. In many cases, the technology just shines a flashlight on the types of issues that adolescents experience—even without a device. Parents should rest assured that a lot of the conversation around phones and well-being is overhyped. If you compare phone use to the effects of lifestyle choices like healthy diets, good sleep, or choosing to use tobacco or alcohol, the effect size is almost zero.

What Happened to the American Childhood? (Julian, 2020)

Children's anxiety is on the rise in the United States, alongside diagnoses of depression, numbers of hospitalizations, and attempts at suicide. What is causing this upward trend in childhood and teenage mental health disorders? Could it be technology? Not likely since young people in nearly every part of the world have access to devices, but this issue of anxious children seems to be particular to the U.S. Psychologists have a different theory, one that has proven itself time and time again. Anxious parents lead to anxious children. Helicopter parents lead to children with high levels of stress. Parents' responses to children's anxiety perpetuate the problem. When parents go out of their way to protect their children from dealing with difficult or uncomfortable situations, children never have an opportunity to develop the coping skills that are so important as they age. Despite research that shows how dangerous helicopter parenting can be, we have a generation of children that is more anxious than ever before. The cure for this dilemma is not just cognitive behavior therapy for the children but the same type of therapy to help parents realize the role they are playing in their child's anxiety and to learn new ways of interacting with that anxiety.

Additional, Related Questions for Students to Explore

1. Does internet addiction exist? How is it similar and different from other forms of addiction?

2. Should technology companies be able to use known psychological methods to turn their customers into habitual users?

3. What is the relationship between feelings of depression, anxiety, and isolation and social media use?

4. Are digital mental health supports giving more people access to help or creating a bigger divide between the "haves and the have nots" in society?

5. When researchers investigate the ties between social media and mental health, is screen time the best indicator to measure? What other factors should researchers consider?

Curricular Connections

Robin Chang (@dangmschang), a high school sociology teacher in Illinois, recently added a new mini-unit to her semester-long class. The intention of the unit was to help students examine their own media habits, the socio-cultural impact of technology being ever-present in our lives, and the ways technology impacts their personal health, wellbeing, and interactions with others.

Inspired by the challenges featured in Manoush Zomorodi's book *Bored and Brilliant* (2017), Chang created a version just for her students and called it "Ms. Chang Breaks the Internet." For one week, students were encouraged to make themselves just a bit uncomfortable by choosing a single challenge from a list and do some simple reflecting over the course of the week.

Ms. Chang offered the following challenges to her student:

1. No photos, please: Focus on capturing memories with your eyes and mind instead.

2. Trash that app: Delete the one app your thumb automatically reaches for when you pick up your phone.

3. In your pocket: Leave your phone out of sight when you are in the presence of another person—choose people over your device.

4. Break the mold: What do people expect to see in your feed? Try acting the opposite and observe how people react. Post a lot of selfies? Try sharing pics of your friends for a change!

5. Pillow talk: Do you usually wind down with your device in your hand? Fall asleep while scrolling? Put your phone out of your reach when you get in bed at night.

6. Call me, maybe?: When was the last time you talked to someone through your phone with your *voice*? Challenge your dependence on text-based messaging apps and try to only communicate with phone calls or FaceTimes.

7. Hey, Alexa . . . : Do you ask your device a million little questions a day? Challenge yourself not to Google answers to your questions for the week. Ask people around you, pick up a book, or consider that maybe ignorance **is** bliss.

Once students (and Ms. Chang!) chose their challenges for the week, they wrote a few sentences about why they made their choice. Each day during the week, students were asked to jot down a few of their thoughts or findings regarding the experiment. The following guiding questions were provided to help students reflect:

1. Is this experiment impacting your mood at all? How so?

2. Are your friends and family treating you differently?

3. Is this experiment improving or negatively impacting your life? Which aspects of it?

4. What has been the hardest part of this challenge?

5. What has pleasantly surprised you during this experiment?

6. Have you accidentally slipped? What caused you to "cheat?" How did you feel afterward?

As the week progressed, Chang watched students move from a state of annoyance about the challenge to the formation of some new habits that the students report made them feel happier and more fulfilled. Many students realized that they had a dependency on communicating through social media, which caused them to be more passively invested in friendships. When they couldn't just watch someone's story or send a quick text, students found that prioritizing other methods of communication and putting in the work to connect with family and friends in a more active way was worth it.

The most surprising part of the project for Ms. Chang? Many students report that they have kept up with their new habits even a year after the project "forced them" to consider their relationships with their device. Now THAT is a successful mini-unit.

Try this

In November of 2019, Instagram announced it would begin hiding the numbers of likes displayed underneath posts. CEO Adam Mosseri said the move was being made to improve the emotional and mental health of users. Instagram was not removing likes completely, but they would become private—meaning you could see how many likes your posts received, but no one else could. And you wouldn't be able to see anyone else's like count either (Yurieff, 2019b).

Using this article as a catalyst for discussion, have small groups of students complete an affinity-mapping activity. The basic structure of this activity is to give students a broad question or problem that could generate a lot of different ideas. You might try, "How can technology companies create

ISTE Standards Addressed

Student Standard 2b: Digital Citizen – Students engage in positive, safe, legal and ethical behavior when using technology, including social interactions online or when using networked devices.

Student Standard 3d: Knowledge Constructor – Students build knowledge by actively exploring real-world issues and problems, developing ideas and theories, and pursuing answers and solutions.

Student Standard 4d: Innovative Designer – Students exhibit a tolerance for ambiguity, perseverance, and the capacity to work with open-ended problems.

Educator Standard 5b: Designer – Design authentic learning activities that align with content area standards and use digital tools and resources to maximize active, deep learning.

Educator Standard 6a: Facilitator – Foster a culture where students take ownership of their learning goals and outcomes in both independent and group settings.

products with mental health concerns in mind?" or "What are the pros and cons of Instagram's decision from the perspective of various stakeholders?" Have students generate responses by writing ideas on sticky notes (one idea per note) and placing them in no particular order on a wall, whiteboard, or chart paper. Alternatively, you could use a Padlet or Google Jamboard to complete this activity digitally.

Once lots of ideas have been generated, have students begin grouping them into similar categories, labeling the categories and discussing why the ideas fit within them, how the categories relate to one another, and so on. Allow students to view other groups' affinity boards or hear a representative from each share their big takeaways. This activity could be followed up with a reflective analysis or a position paper.

More resources

 Scan this QR code for additional articles, resources, and lesson ideas around this question: "What is the relationship between technology and mental health?"

Social Media and Society: Flashlight or Flame?

Early on in my career, I absolutely despised the term "digital citizenship." Everything I read was about controlling student behavior, issuing rules, and making them feel as though the internet was this huge scary place just waiting for them to slip up and make a mistake. It was this fearmongering within the curriculum that motivated me to research the topic for my doctoral dissertation and set me off on a path of redefining the types of conversations adults could be having with kids.

Early in my research, I came across the work of danah boyd. In her 2014 book *It's Complicated: The Social Lives of Networked Teens*, she writes about social media in a way I found so refreshing at the time. The internet was not a place where teens went simply to cause trouble. Not every teen who went online would be lured from their homes and nabbed by a super predator. Screen time was not painted as the epitome of evil and social media was not described as the cause of our social ills. danah boyd was one of the first practical voices I remember reading after digging through piles of digital citizenship curriculum that would lead you to believe the internet was going to be the death of humanity.

Now of course, I have read, written, experienced, and grown a lot in the six years since reading boyd's work and conducting my own deep dive into digital citizenship curriculum. Honestly, the internet is a complicated place. It certainly is not the scary, dangerous, dark alley described in early internet safety curriculum. But it's also not the idyllic, utopian, open space with unlimited access to ideas, people, and information that early adopters hoped it could be.

The reason I bring boyd into this conversation, though, is because it was her work that first got me questioning the relationship between social media and society. In several places in the text, she points out that "social media magnifies many aspects of daily life" (p. 163) and that "the internet mirrors, magnifies, and makes more visible the good, bad, and ugly of everyday life" (p. 24). Her metaphors stood in such sharp contrast to the messages in curriculum and in the news—stories about how technology was destroying our social fabric. Boyd posits that we cannot call social media good or bad because neither of these extremes represent reality.

This chapter is intended to help you and your students wrestle with some of these ideas yourselves. While there are no right or wrong answers, here are a few questions to think about as you read this chapter:

- Is social media causing us to be a more polarized society? Or is it serving as a flashlight, exposing polarization that has always existed?

- Is social media fanning the flames of social unrest or serving as a microphone for the traditionally marginalized?

- Has social media shaped society, or has society shaped social media?

- What obligation do we have to make sure social media platforms are upholding, rather than contributing to, the destruction of democratic ideals?

Building Background Knowledge

I can admit that for a long time, I viewed the internet with unbridled optimism. As a librarian, I wholeheartedly believe that access to information, ideas, and education is a fundamental human right. The internet offers all those things and more. It removes the barriers to information that could

Vocabulary to Know

Partisan polarization – the deviation from balanced political attitudes into ideological extremes; polarization can be a static state describing differences between political parties or other divisions such as religious vs. secular, traditional vs. modern, or rural vs. urban. Polarization can also be a process that refers to an increase in opposing ideas over time.

Meme – cultural units spread from person to person. In the age of the internet, memes often take the form of humorous, satirical, and/or thought-provoking images, videos, or pieces of text or other content that are copied, oftentimes remixed or varied, and spread rapidly by users.

Hashtag – a word or phrase preceded by a # symbol. It is used on social media websites to curate posts and messages on a specific topic into a single thread.

Hashtag activism – also known as social activism or slacktivism, the act of showing support and raising awareness for a cause through social media platforms.

Self-censorship – the act of intentionally withholding one's thoughts out of fear of or respect for the actual or perceived sensibilities of others.

Conspiracy theory – a belief that some covert but influential organization or government is responsible for a circumstance or event.

intentionally or unintentionally exist in physical communities. The internet helps people learn, grow, and find community.

Maybe it is my age or my experience, but I feel as if my rose-colored lenses are getting a bit dirty. The unlimited access to ideas and information that seems so utopian on paper is playing out in some strange, and often unhealthy, ways. Now, I would not say I've turned into a full-on technophobe, but I find myself asking more critical questions these days. Questions about whether every voice deserves an equally loud microphone and about whether a system of peer review before publication needs to happen online too. <Sigh>

I don't have the answers to these questions—none of us really do—but I find it important to reflect on our own biases and perspectives before diving into some potentially messy conversations. Recognizing where my own thinking currently lies and how it has developed over time helps me be more open to the perspectives and thoughts of others. See if you can find elements of your own thinking in the schools of thought presented next.

Technological utopia

The term *utopia* is used to describe a perfect society. In fiction, the presence of utopias is supposed to help us ask questions such as: What if we didn't value wealth or social status? What if no one had to go without? What if we never had to fight or go to war? Technological utopianism is an ideology that proposes that advances in science and technology could bring about a utopia—an ideal society where every formal structure that exists is exclusively operating for the benefit and well-being of all citizens.

In the early days of the internet, tech-utopianism drove innovation. The internet was described as a superhighway, a marketplace of ideas, a modern-day printing press, a liberation from the gatekeepers. Silicon Valley was ready to "move fast and break things."

Mark Zuckerberg, founder of Facebook, and his roommate Chris Hughes would often talk about how wiring the world was going to be one of the most important ways to change it. In 2018, Zuckerberg posted a note on his Facebook profile that summed up his views rather neatly: "Many of us got into technology because we believe it can be a democratizing force for putting power in people's hands. I believe the world is better when more people have a voice to share their experiences, and when traditional gatekeepers such as governments and media companies don't control what ideas can be expressed" (as cited in Marantz, 2019).

Technological utopianism has moved beyond the goals of connecting the world, and now proponents see new technologies such as AR/VR, drones, 3D printing, blockchain, and bitcoin as the types of products that will help bring about systemic, societal change (Taneja, 2019).

Technological dystopia

If you have read the work of Ray Bradbury or caught a few episodes of *Black Mirror* on Netflix, you've been exposed to the ideas of a technological dystopia. Typically, a fictional dystopia will present extreme and disturbing answers to the same questions explored in fictional utopias, which present the best-case outcomes. Many people claim the type of technological utopianism that led to the creation of the major tech giants we have today is dead, and that we are moving toward a reality that looks much more dystopian.

Removing the information gatekeepers, it turns out, leads to hate speech, misinformation, and the warping of content to benefit politicians and corporations. Technology recreated the way we communicate and socialize, and out of thin air, we displaced systems and structures that took hundreds of years to put into place. Instead of giving power to the people, technology has taken their data and privacy and put it in the hands of a few very wealthy and immensely powerful people and companies.

Not all creators stuck around for the ride, though. Many even jumped off the techno-utopian bandwagon altogether. Both 4chan and 8chan (now 8kun), unregulated and unrestrained discussion boards that allow users to post anonymously, have been described as the underbellies of the internet. The creators of each company have walked away entirely, and they are now owned by other people. Fredrick Brennan, who created 8chan and abandoned it in 2016, has watched horrifying and depressing things happen in the space, including the radicalization of young people and white-supremacists plots that developed online and turned into acts of violence. In an interview with *The New Yorker*, Brennan said, "If I could, I'd delete 8chan in a second. It's way beyond the point of no return" (Marantz, 2019).

Techno-optimism and techno-pragmatism

We do not have to see technology as purely utopian or dystopian. There are some ideologies that lie in the center.

Techno-optimism is the recognition of the faults with technology balanced with a healthy optimism about the future of it. Cory Doctorow, a Canadian blogger, journalist, and science fiction writer, says that we must be pessimistic enough about technology to recognize that things can get worse if they go unchecked, but we must also believe that if we take the proper course of action, the worst is preventable. To him, techno-optimism is "an ideology that embodies [pessimism and optimism]: the concern that technology could be used to make the world worse, the hope that it can be steered to make the world better" (as cited in Barnard, 2019).

Techno-pragmatism is a more specific, practical extension of the techno-optimism described above. The core tenets of techno-pragmatism are that technology should be designed to create value for the user, not for the shareholder. Techno-pragmatists believe that the purpose of technology is to improve life, that new tech is not automatically the best answer, that the impacts of new technology on social behaviors and norms should be assessed before adoption. They also believe that technology is a magnifier that will "dramatically scale both good and bad human interactions and intent" (Rolston, 2019).

Breaking Down the Arguments

There is a common phrase in the library world that says books are "windows, mirrors, and sliding glass doors." Great library collections should allow students to find themselves within the pages on the shelves, view parts of the world that they haven't been able to before, and find books that invite them to step into the shoes of other people and imagine their experiences.

I could draw a similar comparison to the internet and social media. Through these mediums, we can find other people who think, look, behave, or generally experience the world in the same ways that we do. We can also see and experience aspects of life that are unlike our own. But what happens when the things we see are not pretty? When what we witness through the window shocks us? Makes us feel angry, ashamed, or depressed? Is it the window's fault? Or has the ugliness always been there?

In this section, we will examine several different claims about the role of social media in our society. Is it a mirror of who we are or a flashlight exposing the parts we've long ignored? Perhaps social media is something entirely different—a flame slowly warming a pot of water to its boiling point?

Claim #1: Social media has created more political and social division.

Social media has inflamed political and social divisions. People who support this claim are likely to point out that:

- People surround themselves with others who think the way they do. There is a level of camaraderie and reinforcement of beliefs within the group; members' ideas are rarely challenged.

- People become victims of confirmation bias. They seek out accounts, news sources, journalists, and politicians to follow who can confirm their own thinking.

- Social media dehumanizes interactions and makes it easier to argue than compromise.

What the research says

Do online platforms like Twitter create more political polarization because of the echo chambers people choose to engage in, or does social media help create more interactions with people of varying political views because of the openness of the internet and the vast number of ideas and opinions available for public consumption? One study tested this idea by analyzing the Twitter accounts of politicians from the U.S. House of Representatives. Research indicated that politicians with more extreme ideological positions had higher levels of Twitter readerships and reach than their moderate peers. A large body of research in the e-government literature has tracked the growing number of ways that politicians collect ideas and opinions from their constituents due to the ease of communication. However, online platforms tend to collect and integrate the voices of constituents that are already within the echo chamber and not outside of it. If the systems by which information is collected and disseminated are already biased toward extreme positions rather than moderate ones, Twitter has the potential to contribute to partisan polarization (Hong & Kim, 2016).

Another way that social media influences and contributes to partisan polarization is through an interesting feedback loop. In a 2018 study, researchers Wihbey, Joseph, and Lazer posed the question, "What is the relationship between the partisan leaning of a journalists' social network on Twitter and the news content he or she produces?" After an analysis of both the Twitter activity of and the articles produced by 644 journalists from 25 news outlets, the researchers found a significant correlation "between the ideological character of a journalist's social network and ideological dimensions of his or her published output, even when controlling for the outlet for which the journalist writes." The connection between agendas on social media and those that emerge from publications by mass media outlets suggests an odd, cyclical paradox by which journalists take their cues from a steady social media diet and then turn around to develop even more polarizing and sometimes sensational content to keep feeding the polarization we see in digital communities today.

In the news

'Pure Negativity': Division over Pandemic Creates Challenges, Opportunities in Rural Facebook Groups (2020)

Kristie Spotts Cobbley is a moderator of a Facebook group in rural Colorado. She created a bulletin board group for her community in 2012 and has been able to take a somewhat hands-off approach to moderating the space where people will ask for recommendations about home repairs or post announcements about lost pets. That is, until recently. Soon after Walmart announced that shoppers would be required to wear masks to help prevent the spread of COVID-19, the 5,600-member group turned ugly.

Cobbley felt she had no choice but to take back some control in what started to feel like a digital battleground. She left many informational posts but had to close the comments sections. She also had to revisit the basic "be nice" rules that had guided the community for nearly eight years and replace them with much more specific dos and don'ts for conduct that could be reinforced without bias. Cobbey says the work of moderating such division has taken a toll on her emotionally, and there are times she doesn't even want to look at the group. And while Cobbey says she's willing to endure this rough patch and keep her community group open, others have chosen a different path.

In another rural community about an hour and a half away from Cobbey's town, a 9,600- member Facebook group recently deactivated. The moderator, Kate Kenney, says that over the years she has seen political debate and negativity rise to an unbearable level. She said running the group became like a full-time job, and it was affecting her personal relationships and her mental health. Even though good things were accomplished over the years through the group—the restoration of a local cemetery, for example—Kenney says that with all of the division around COVID and the current political climate, keeping the group open just didn't feel worth it.

COVID-19 Doesn't Care About Our Political Divide. In Pandemic, We Need to Work Together (Darling, 2020)

Everyone in the United States can agree that the COVID-19 pandemic has been politicized. What we cannot seem to agree on is who it is that's done the politicizing. Republicans are blaming Democrats for overreacting about the virus because it is an election year. Democrats accuse Republicans of valuing the economy more than people's lives. Unfortunately, many journalists fuel the flames of division by comparing infection and death rates in blue versus red states. When bias, sensationalism, and finger-pointing drown out voices of reason, even something as neutral as a virus, that should be uniting citizens in a fight against a common enemy, has turned into a tool for social division.

But it isn't just the politicians and journalists who are politicizing these issues. On the internet, we seek out and share sources that confirm our own beliefs. We want to feel as though we are on the "right" side of the argument, so we are quick to skim the details, share the headlines, and argue with our friends, all in an effort to prove the rightness of our opinions. But our divisions can be dangerous, so we need less finger-pointing and more cooperation and collaboration if we want to come out of this difficult time as stronger individuals and as stronger communities.

Claim #2: Social media does not reflect the real America.

People who take up claim #1 believe that social media has, in fact, made our society more divided than ever, but there is another argument about how social media serves as a flame. This argument is different, but in a very nuanced way. Claim #1 argues we are worse off as a society than we have ever been because of social media. People who support claim #2, however, say that our society has *not* gotten worse, but that the activity we see on social media has duped us into thinking we have. The perception of extreme division, however, is still problematic in and of itself.

Has social media simply enflamed us into *believing* our society is at a breaking point? People who say "yes" will point out that:

- Social media amplifies the loudest voices, not the most even-keeled.

- Social media has many passive consumers of content who choose not to actively share.

- Much of what we see on social media is driven by profit.

What the research says

A new national survey finds that self-censorship is on the rise in the United States. Sixty-two percent of Americans say that the current political climate is preventing them from expressing their political beliefs for fear of offending others or fear of retaliation like getting fired from a job or missing out on a career advancement opportunity. This number is up from 58% of Americans who reported levels of self-censoring in a 2017 survey.

Self-censorship is widespread amongst a variety of demographics, including political party affiliation. Sixty-five percent of Latinx Americans, 64% of White Americans, and 49% of Black Americans all report they have political views they are afraid to share. The numbers were also close to equal when sorting by gender (65% of males and 59% of females), income level (60% with incomes over $100,000 and 58% with incomes under $20,000), and age (55% of people under 35 and 66% of people over 65), and political party (52% of self-identified Democrats, 59% of self-identified Independents, and 77% of self-identified Republicans).

The survey also included questions to help researchers label participants as strong liberal, liberal, moderate, conservative, and strong conservative. They found that 64% of respondents who report being too afraid to share their political beliefs were from the politically moderate category. This means there is a large population of voices who may have the type of balanced, compromised policy ideas we desperately need, but because they are not put out into the public sphere, there is no real opportunity for others to understand, scrutinize, reform, or adopt them (Ekins, 2020).

This self-censoring of ideas leads to a skewed picture of where we are politically as a country. When we look at social media, we see the voices of the most extreme ends of the political spectrum, not the more moderate majority that is choosing to disengage from the conversation. Perhaps the flame has been made so big, we've scared a lot of voices away.

This idea certainly coincides with the work of Salena Zito, a U.S. political reporter who researches and writes about American politics. She and colleague Brad Todd traveled over 27,000 miles to interview more than 300 Trump supporters in 10 different states to try to figure out how so many political experts wrongly predicted the 2016 election results. In a 2019 piece for the *Washington Examiner*, Zito talks about what she's learned about the role social media plays in politics. In her experiences, social media is more of a silencer than it is a political town hall. Unfortunately, both extreme ends of the political spectrum feel they hold the ultimate truth even though the foundation of democracy is that no one holds absolute truth, so we must come together to continuously get better. But when moderates passively observe social media and stay quiet about their political differences for fear of attack, Twitter cannot possibly reflect real life.

As Zito points out, can you imagine walking down the street carrying a cup of coffee someone finds politically offensive, so they begin publicly yelling and calling you a bigot? How crazy would our world look if a mob attacked you in the street for smiling at a joke they find to be delivered in poor taste? Essentially, Zito says that Twitter and other social media communities are not reflective of the human-level communities we thrive in.

In the news

The Troll: A Fake Flag Burning at Gettysburg Was Only His Latest Hoax (Boburg & Bennett, 2020)

This *Washington Post* piece introduces readers to Adam Rahuba, a thirty-eight-year-old DJ and food-delivery driver who is the anonymous figure behind several large social media hoaxes. Rahuba claims he creates these hoaxes mostly to entertain himself, rile up far-right extremists, and prove how "gullible" people are about the things they see online. His latest hoax was an advertised Fourth of July flag burning event at a cemetery in Gettysburg, PA. The only people that showed up to the event, though, were "counter-protestors" who arrived flying both American and Confederate flags while also brandishing weapons. In a similar hoax he initiated in 2017, an armed counter-protestor shot himself in the leg with his own revolver. Similarly, bystanders have been harassed and attacked when counter-protestors assume that if you are not with them, you must clearly be there to burn a flag.

Rahuba admits to running intentionally controversial websites that earn money through ads and high traffic to the site. For a time, he ran a site called 911wasfunny.com that spread messages like "those pompous NY people deserved to die." He has also run a site proposing a "Trayvon Martin" amendment that would change the constitution to do away with the Second Amendment in honor of the life of Trayvon. Salacious headlines that called the NRA out as a terrorist organization were quickly shared and debated on social media, bringing more traffic to the site and resulting in more money for Rahuba. He has also earned money by selling T-shirts with divisive messages and by creating sob stories and fake identities for GoFundMe campaigns.

Rahuba admits that "controversy creates cash," but it also creates the perception of extreme polarization and partisanship in our country when you see Rahuba's hoaxes go viral. Instead of true extremism by members of our society, we are seeing chaos crafted for a profit.

Are Conspiracy Theories on the Rise in the US? (Vittert, 2020)

Conspiracy theories abound on the internet. People talk about everything from the "deep state" working against President Trump to 9/11 being an inside job. Have you heard the one about vapor trails left by aircraft actually being chemical agents sprayed by our government officials? Or what about stores encouraging debit and credit transactions during the COVID pandemic being a secret plot to move toward a cashless society?

Seeing all of the chatter out there might make you feel as though you're the only sane person left who doesn't think everything in life is actually a plot by the government to harm you or take away your freedoms. But is that reality? Not according to historical data. There is not a lot of formal polling on Americans' beliefs in conspiracy theories prior to the year 2000, but based on 120 years of letters to the editor from both *The New York Times* and the *Chicago Tribune*, it appears that there has been absolutely no change in the amount of conspiracy theory belief over time.

This isn't the first time Americans have felt surrounded by conspiracy theories. During major innovations in media—the printing press, mass publishing, the radio, and cable television—researchers and the public have historically proclaimed it was also the dawn of a new age of conspiracy theories. Although the internet has made it easier for people to discuss conspiracy theories, there is no evidence to suggest that belief in these theories has increased.

Claim #3: Hashtag activism has raised awareness of social injustices.

People who believe the internet has been a powerful tool for shining a light on the injustices of society are likely to support that claim with the following arguments:

- Social media allows the marginalized and historically voiceless to tell their stories.

- The barriers to communication between "everyday people" and politicians, celebrities, and other influencers have greatly diminished.

- Because of social media, more people have been exposed to these injustices, allowing for a critical mass to demand action.

What the research says

A 2016 study from the Center for Media and Social Impact examined the effectiveness of the Black Lives Matter hashtag in starting a nationwide conversation about police killings of unarmed Black citizens. Although the #BlackLivesMatter hashtag was created in July 2013 after the unarmed shooting of Trayvon Martin in Sanford, Florida, it really picked up steam and become a more significant movement in the months following protests in Ferguson, Missouri, over the fatal shooting of Michael Brown by police.

The study included an analysis of more than 40 million tweets by more than 4 million unique users that were publicly made between June 1, 2014, and May 31, 2015. Not only were the tweets themselves part of the dataset, but the researchers also pulled links, videos, and images from the tweets to analyze. The purpose of the investigation was to see how far the #BlackLivesMatter conversation had spread, who was engaging in the conversation, and whether the conversation was successful at bringing about awareness or change.

The major findings of this study indicate that social media posts by activists were essential in spreading the conversation nationally. According to interviews with activists, the primary goal of using social media was to educate the greater community, amplify marginalized voices, and advocate for structural police reform. Evidence from the year of tweets suggests that the activists were successful in educating casual observers because as the year progressed, more unique accounts started joining the conversation.

However, the study found that activists might be somewhat limited in the extent to which they can generate large scale online debate by themselves. Once more influential accounts, such as those of Black celebrities and politicians, began using the hashtag, the bigger the conversation grew. It is important to note, though, that throughout the year, the Twitter discussion remained Black-led (Freelon et al., 2016).

Since the time of the study, the #BlackLivesMatter hashtag has been used as a rallying cry to activists time and time again and has been used to rally voices and protestors in a number of police brutality cases, including the recent deaths of Breonna Taylor and George Floyd.

In the news

How Trump and the Black Lives Matter Movement Changed White Voters' Minds (Herndon & Searcey, 2020)

Recent surveys across the U.S. indicate that people across races, places, and age brackets have been awakened to the complaints Black Americans have been making about police brutality and systemic racism for decades. Samuel Sinyangwe, an activist and cofounder of Mapping Police Violence, has said a lot of his work has been centered around convincing those outside of the Black community that there is an actual problem. The death of George Floyd at the hands of the Minneapolis Police Department, the resulting protests across the country, and President Trump's calls for more "law and order" certainly seem to have tipped the scales. Fifty-nine percent of voters, including 52% of white voters, believe that there is a pattern of excessive police violence toward African Americans, and many are ready to have difficult conversations.

Nell Irvin Painter, a historian and author, says that our country has had a great stalling point after the civil rights movement. White Americans thought racism had ended and avoided talking about race for a long time. Now, many white people are stepping up and saying it is time to talk about whiteness and privilege and stand beside our Black brothers and sisters to make change happen.

7 Positive Changes That Have Come From the #MeToo Movement
(North, 2019)

The #MeToo movement was intended to help survivors of sexual assault feel as though they were not alone. The movement gained attention beyond the survivor community too, and it started a nationwide conversation about sexual assault and abuse. Here are just a few of the ways a hashtag has initiated change.

Aside from powerful men like Harvey Weinstein and Matt Lauer losing their jobs and facing charges, there are some broader, society-level changes being made as well. Several states are banning nondisclosure agreements that silence victims of sexual harassment with money if they promise to stay quiet. Others are introducing more protections for independent contractors, domestic workers, and gig workers who have not historically had the same protections from workplace harassment as full-time employees. There has also been a movement to end the tipped minimum wage. Restaurant workers, bartenders, and others who rely mainly on tips as their source of income often report tolerating harassment from customers for fear of losing money if they speak up against it.

To help women with the costs of filing sexual harassment lawsuits, a group of women in Hollywood started the Time's Up Legal Defense Fund to help women obtain legal representation. To date, it has raised more than $25 million and has connected nearly 4,000 survivors with attorneys. Some survivors, like the athletes who spoke out against USA Gymnastics team doctor Larry Nassar, are looking at financial restitution because of their lawsuits.

Overall, Americans are changing their attitudes about sexual assault. There is more trust in victims' stories, more willingness to question those in power, and more open dialogue about the lasting impacts of sexual harassment on survivors.

Claim #4: Meme culture reveals what we value.

When was the last time you flipped open a newspaper to read a political cartoon? How about the last time you stopped to ponder a piece of statement art? For centuries, the nation's shortcomings as well as our human flaws have been gently (and sometimes not so gently) exposed to us through these simple yet thought-provoking pieces of media. Today, those thought-provoking media pieces tend to come in the form of an internet meme.

People who believe that memes and other viral content serve as a flashlight in our society may cite arguments such as:

- Memes are easy to create and publish, allowing anyone to share their story or perspective.

- Memes can be easily duplicated, modified, and spread again, adding nuance to the conversation.

- Content that "goes viral" indicates what we value as a society.

What the research says

A meme is easy to make, but there is no guarantee that the simple act of creating one will lead to its going "viral." Much like the market principles that dictate trends in clothing, the success of a movie, and the popularity of music, a meme is competing for attention in a huge marketplace of other content. In most economic systems, we can measure the relative success of a product based on supply, demand, distribution, and price points. In memes and other viral content, though, the feedback loop from the audience to the creator happens through social scrutiny, remixing, resampling, and resharing of ideas, resulting in millions of trial-and-error experiments to grab the attention of the masses. Memes that are interpreted by the audience as having a strong message worthy of communicating take hold and proliferate. When users see no value in the messages—whether they are too boring, too controversial, or simply unclear—they fade into oblivion (Tippens, 2017).

For content to go viral, it must embrace a component of our shared societal values and cultural experiences. Some of the most popular memes today include images of Willy Wonka, characters from *The Office*, SpongeBob SquarePants, Will Ferrell, Michael Jackson, Michael Jordan, Kermit the Frog, and other recognizable pop icons. The use of these shared cultural icons in memes can invoke feelings of nostalgia, shared experiences, and social validation, all of which contribute to their virality, reinforce the shared culture, and reflect our shared interests (Guadagno et al., 2013).

Memes can also reflect shared values within smaller communities. In social media forums and groups, when memes are consistent with the themes, beliefs, or stances of that group, they spread at a much higher rate than memes that are inconsistent with the purposes of the group. This holds true even when accounting for the popularity or status of the initial meme sharer (Mazambani et al., 2015).

In the same way memes can show us what we have in common, the virality of hurtful memes shines a bright flashlight on who we do and do not value in society. What does it say about our social values to have a "People of Walmart" Facebook page that seeks to identify and mock those that are poorly dressed, less educated, living in poverty, or in other ways part of the "out-group?" In a critical discourse analysis of memes that center around socioeconomic status, researchers Dobson and Knezevic (2017) found that memes used to describe the poor were derogatory, stereotypical, condescending, and full of victim blaming. Common themes that emerged from the eighty-five memes depicting poor people that included the "lazy welfare recipient," who refuses to work in order to game the system; the "punitive of the poor" perspective, in which people put additional hoops or conditions on the poor like, "you should have to get drug tested to get food stamps"; and the "undeserving poor" memes, in which the non-poor pass judgment on the less fortunate with messages such as: "News flash; if you are home with your kids but are getting a check from the government, you are NOT a stay-at-home mom. You are unemployed and leeching off the system—go get a job!" (Dobson & Knezevic, 2017).

Whether today's hottest viral content is funny and lighthearted or full of vitriol over a current event, memes are like a digital time capsule of our attitudes, shared beliefs, and collective discourse during any given period of time.

In the news

#Distractinglysexy Tweets Are Female Scientists' Retort to 'Disappointing' Comments (Chappell, 2015)

Nobel Prize–winning biochemist Tim Hunt made remarks at an international conference that the problem with having women in the science lab is that "you fall in love with them, they fall in love with you, and when you criticize them, they cry."

Female scientists quickly took to social media to point out the ridiculousness of Hunt's statement by posting pictures of their #DistractinglySexy selves in lab goggles, biohazard suits, and in the field covered with mud to make an ironic point. Others shared memes, such as a sign that read, "CAUTION: MIXED GENDER LAB! NO FALLING IN LOVE OR CRYING PERMITTED." The women who work in science say the hashtag is being used to point out the ridiculousness of Hunt's statement and to bring visibility to the number of women working hard in scientific fields every day.

A Brief History of 'Karen' (Goldblatt, 2020)

Once a popular name for girls born in the 1960s, the name Karen has since become synonymous with a middle-aged busybody who asks to speak to the manager. Even more recently, the name has been morphed into a symbol of white privilege.

A "Karen" is now someone who is incessantly aggrieved, hellbent on tattling on people—typically people of color—and often behaving as though their lives are more valuable than anyone else's. Recent examples of "Karens" include a white woman who was caught on film demanding immigration papers from her neighbor's landscaper, another who threatened to call the police on a Black child who was selling water to people near a park, and yet another who called the police on a Filipino man stenciling "Black Lives Matter" on his own property!

Historians point out that the notion of a "Karen" is not new, even though the term has changed. During the antebellum and Jim Crow periods, Black Americans typically used the term "Miss Ann" to refer to unreasonable

> ## Additional, Related Questions for Students to Explore
>
> 1. Is viral content an accurate reflection of who we are as a society?
>
> 2. Does the internet cause and promote uncivil behavior or is it simply putting our natural incivility on stage for all to see?
>
> 3. Should creators of viral content be compensated for their work?

white women who would go to any and all lengths to uphold their place in the upper end of the societal hierarchy.

Some women actually named Karen have voiced outrage over the meme, but many of them support its use because of the messaging behind it. One San Francisco Bay Area–woman, Karen Chang, said, "I would sacrifice my name for the visibility and awareness [these incidents] generate."

Curricular Connections

In conducting research for this book, it was difficult to find educators who were already broaching these topics in the classroom. Perhaps this is because we lack curricular resources to do so, or maybe it is because we adults still don't fully understand the extent to which social media manipulates us.

In the fall of 2020, Netflix released *The Social Dilemma*, a documentary-drama hybrid that explores the human and societal impact of social media. The film features current and former employees of major tech companies, including Google and Facebook. They lead viewers down a path from the business and money-making side of social media to the very real, unintended outcomes these algorithms have had on society and democracy.

ISTE Standards Addressed

Student Standard 1d: Empowered Learner – Students understand the fundamental concepts of technology operations, demonstrate the ability to choose, use and troubleshoot current technologies and are able to transfer their knowledge to explore emerging technologies.

Student Standard 3d: Knowledge Constructor – Students build knowledge by actively exploring real-world issues and problems, developing ideas and theories and pursuing answers and solutions.

Educator Standard 6a: Facilitator – Foster a culture where students take ownership of their learning goals and outcomes in both independent and group settings.

Educator Standard 6d: Facilitator – Model and nurture creativity and creative expression to communicate ideas, knowledge, or connections.

This documentary can serve as an important curricular resource for students in grades eight through twelve. The accompanying website includes conversation tools, bonus clips, technology challenges, and planning materials to help you either debrief this information in the classroom or even hold a community event to bring awareness to adults too!

Scan the QR code to access these resources.

Try this

Pyramid discussions, also known as snowball discussions, are a great way to cover a lot of ground and help all students have an active part in the conversation. In the basic structure, students begin in pairs, responding to a discussion question only to one another. Then the pair joins another pair, and there is a discussion amongst four students. Then two groups of four become a discussion group of eight. This continues until the whole class is joined up in one large discussion.

There are a lot of variations on this activity as well. You could toss a single question out to the class that continues to get batted around each time the groups merge. Or, you could have some more specific questions in the beginning, and each time the groups change, the question gets a little broader. You could also conduct a reverse snowball or pyramid where the whole class starts the discussion together and you slowly break into smaller groups until everyone ends up in pairs.

Any of the questions you read throughout this chapter would make for excellent classroom discussions around technology's relationship with society.

More resources

 Scan this QR code for additional articles, resources, and lesson ideas around this question: "Has social media changed us, or is it simply a reflection of who we are?"

Conclusion and Call to Action

As I am writing the conclusion to this book, the world is in a bizarre place.

Several months into the COVID-19 pandemic, schools across the United States look quite different than they ever have before. Some children are in classrooms wearing masks and socially distancing. Others are learning remotely, and still more are doing a blend of each. Families are juggling a mix of unusual work and school schedules as we collectively hold our breath, waiting to see what the COVID-19 pandemic is going to bring next.

During the summer of 2020, our country witnessed the death of George Floyd at the hands of the Minneapolis Police Department. People across the country risked exposure to a deadly virus to take to the streets in protest, and a national conversation around not only police brutality but all forms of systemic racism ensued.

But the conversations have not been easy. They have not been cordial. In August, a 17- year-old boy named Kyle Rittenhouse crossed state lines with a rifle to protect businesses from riots but ended up fatally shooting two men and injuring a third. In October, 14 men associated with a far-right militia group were charged with plotting to kidnap the governor of Michigan, Gretchen Whitmer. This news followed ongoing protests from Republicans in the state regarding COVID-19 restrictions there.

Last week, President-Elect Joe Biden and Vice President–Elect Kamala Harris made history, not only in the number of votes they received but also because our country now has a woman of color in the White House. Unfortunately, this tremendous step in equality for women has been overshadowed by accusations of voter fraud from the sitting President Trump, who has yet to deliver a concession speech.

Throughout this crazy, tumultuous year, social media has been a stage to showcase all of the ugliness and division in our country. Every day we tune into arguments over masks and vaccines, in-person versus remote schooling, the legitimacy of our democratic processes and how much we can trust science, our government, and one another. It all feels like too much to handle. While mainstream platforms like Twitter and Facebook are making strides to put content warnings on misinformation, and media giants are calling out shenanigans when they see them, there are people who feel this correction of misinformation is somehow a form of censorship. So, we see new apps like Parler and fringe networks like NewsMax promising users to give them the freedom to share or consume the types of sensationalized content they seem to prefer.

Admittedly, by the time this book is in my hands or yours, so much of what I have said here will be old news. We will have sworn in a new president. There may be more promising solutions to COVID-19 on the horizon. Perhaps some of our anger and vitriol will diminish, but it is also possible that our collective attention spans will be drawn into new debates and new concerns—ones I cannot even imagine right now.

And yet, through the mess of it all, one constant remains, even in 2020: our humanity. Over the course of history, we have witnessed how humans evolve and grow through conflict, heartache, and struggle. When difficulties come our way, it is our collective commitment as a human race to pick ourselves up, dust ourselves off, and work toward a brighter future that gifts the generations after ours with a better world.

I believe it is our duty as educators to equip the next generation with the words, the tools, and the opportunities to wade around in the struggles and recognize that the flaws in the technology we use every day really can shape us as a society. Our students will face their fair share of societal growing pains, and engaging them in conversations like the ones presented in this text will better prepare them to think critically, consider multiple points of view, and find ways to move us forward in a more equitable manner.

Aside from the resources I've mentioned already in this book, I'd like to recommend some content that can help you think more critically about the technology in your life. Educators are lifelong learners, and the more we expand our understanding of various topics, the better equipped we are to help students do the same. So, if you are hungry for more, check out the lists below. (Scan the QR code for easy access to each of these resources.)

Listen:

- *Note to Self* with Manoush Zomorodi
- *Rabbit Hole* from *The New York Times*
- *Reply All* with PJ Vogt and Alex Goldman
- *Should This Exist?* hosted by Caterina Fake
- *Why'd You Push That Button* from The Verge

Watch:

- *The American Meme* (2018)
- *Black Mirror* (2011)
- *Eighth Grade* (2018)
- *The Social Dilemma* (2020)
- *Terms and Conditions May Apply* (2013)

Read:

- *Automating Inequality* by Virginia Eubanks (2017)
- *Algorithms of Oppression* by Safiya Umoja Noble (2018)
- *Behind the Screen* by Sarah T. Roberts (2019)
- *Bored and Brilliant* by Manoush Zomorodi (2017)
- *Weapons of Math Destruction* by Cathy O'Neal (2016)

While the world is certainly at a messy turning point, my parting words to you are these: Don't despair. Educators and families are having amazing, critical conversations right now about long-standing traditions in education whose flaws have become hyper-visible as we've moved our classrooms online. Political officials, tech companies, lawyers, and historians are having crucial conversations about the role of social media, misinformation, and disinformation on civic engagement and democratic principles. People from various industries and backgrounds are asking important questions about how the tools at our fingertips enhance our humanity or strip it away.

Don't shy away from these conversations. Don't tune them out. Embrace the messy. Play around in the gray areas. Question your assumptions—not just in your use of technology but in life. And then, once you've gotten comfortable in the nebulous world of digital ethics, invite your students into a safe space where they can explore these tough questions too.

References

Abedjan, Z., Boujemaa, N., Campbell, S., Casla, P., Chatterjea, S., Consoli, S., . . . Wuyts, R. (2019). Data science in healthcare: Benefits, challenges and opportunities. In Consoli S., Reforgiato Recupero D., & Petković M. (Eds.). *Data science for healthcare* (3–28). Springer. https://doi.org/10.1007/978-3-030-05249-2_1

American Psychiatric Association. (2013). *Diagnostic and statistical manual of mental disorders* (5th ed.).

Anderson, J., & Rainie, L. (2017, October 19). The future of truth and misinformation online. Pew Research Center. http://www.elon.edu/docs/e-web/imagining/surveys/2017_survey/Future_of_Info_Environment_Elon_University_Pew_10-18-17.pdf

Andersson, H. (2018, July 04). Social media apps are 'deliberately' addictive to users. BBC News. https://www.bbc.com/news/technology-44640959

Andorfer, A. (2018). Spreading like wildfire: Solutions for abating the fake news problem on social media via technology controls and government regulation. *Hastings Law Journal, 69*(5), 1409–1431. https://repository.uchastings.edu/hastings_law_journal/vol69/iss5/5

Anzilotti, E. (2019, February 19). Gig economy platform Thumbtack is helping its users get benefits. Fast Company. https://www.fastcompany.com/90308307/gig-economy-platform-thumbtack-is-helping-its-users-get-benefits

Arthur, R. (2019, July 10). We analyzed more than 1 million comments on 4chan. Hate speech there has spiked by 40% since 2015. Vice News. https://www.vice.com/en_us/article/d3nbzy/we-analyzed-more-than-1-million-comments-on-4chan-hate-speech-there-has-spiked-by-40-since-2015

Atieno, E. (2017, February 26). Damn, Daniel: White mediocrity wins again. HuffPost. https://www.huffpost.com/entry/damn-daniel-white-mediocrit_b_9328438

Automation in the workplace. (2019). *Gale In Context: Opposing Viewpoints*. Farmington Hills, MI: Gale. https://link.gale.com/apps/doc/EGQZET067005876/OVIC?u=nape28931&sid=OVIC&xid=b7bcfa08

Barnard, M. (2019, October 17). A manifesto for pragmatic techno-optimism. Medium. medium.com/the-future-is-electric/a-manifesto-for-pragmatic-techno-optimism-50dd3f6372bc

Blodget, H (2009, October 1). Mark Zuckerberg on innovation. Business Insider. https://www.businessinsider.com/mark-zuckerberg-innovation-2009-10

Boburg, S., & Bennett, D. (2020, July 17). The Troll: A fake flag burning at Gettysburg was only his latest hoax. *The Washington Post*. https://www.washingtonpost.com/investigations/2020/07/17/gettysburg-antifa-flag-burning-troll/?arc404=true

Bousquet, C. (2017, February 28). Ten ways cities are nudging for better, healthier citizens. Data-Smart City Solutions. https://datasmart.ash.harvard.edu/news/article/ten-ways -cities-are-nudging-for-better-healthier-citizens-986

boyd, d. (2014). *It's complicated: The social lives of networked teens.* Yale University Press.

Broussard, M. (2018). *Artificial unintelligence: How computers misunderstand the world.* The MIT Press.

CBC Radio. (2018, November 24). 'Alexa, who did it?' What happens when a judge in a murder trial wants data from a smart home speaker. https://www.cbc.ca/radio/day6/ episode-417-alexa-as-murder-witness-k-tel-s-legacy-brexit-and-gibraltar-havana-s -mystery-hater-and-more-1.4916536/alexa-who-did-it-what-happens-when-a-judge -in-a-murder-trial-wants-data-from-a-smart-home-speaker-1.4916556

Ceccato, V. (2019). Eyes and apps on the streets: From surveillance to sousveillance using smartphones. *Criminal Justice Review, 44*(1), 25–41. https://doi.org/ 10.1177/0734016818818696

Centers for Disease Control and Prevention. (2020, June 15). Data and statistics on children's mental health. https://www.cdc.gov/childrensmentalhealth/data.html

Chafey, D. (2020, June 1). What happens online in 60 seconds? [Infographic]. Smart Insights. https://www.smartinsights.com/internet-marketing-statistics/happens- online-60-seconds

Chappell, B. (2015, June 12). #Distractinglysexy tweets are female scientists' retort to 'disappointing' comments. NPR. https://www.npr.org/sections/thetwo- way/2015/06/12/413986529/-distractinglysexy-tweets-are-female-scientists-retort-to -disappointing-comments

Chowdhury, M., & Sadek, A. W. (2012). Advantages and limitations of artificial intelligence. *Artificial Intelligence Applications to Critical Transportation Issues, Transportation Research Circular, E-C168,* 6–8. http://www.trb.org/Main/ Blurbs/168134.aspx

Collaborative for Academic, Social, and Emotional Learning (CASEL). (2020). SEL: What Are the Core Competence Areas and Where are they Promoted? https://casel.org/sel -framework

Collins, B. (2020, February 21). Twitter is testing new ways to fight misinformation— including a community-based points system. NBC News. https://www.nbcnews .com/tech/tech-news/twitter-testing-new-ways-fight-misinformation-including -community-based-points-n1139931

Collins, K., & Dance, G. J. (2018, March 20). How researchers learned to use Facebook 'likes' to sway your thinking. *The New York Times.* https://www.nytimes.com/2018/03/ 20/technology/facebook-cambridge-behavior-model.html

Convertino, J. (2020, March 5). Social media companies partnering with health authorities to combat misinformation on coronavirus. ABC News. https://abcnews .go.com/Technology/social-media-companies-partnering-health-authorities-combat -misinformation/story?id=69389222

Cowgill, B. (2020, March 21). *Bias and productivity in humans and algorithms: Theory and evidence from résumé screening.* Columbia University. http://conference.iza.org/ conference_files/MacroEcon_2017/cowgill_b8981.pdf

Coyne, S. M., Rogers, A. A., Zurcher, J. D., Stockdale, L., & Booth, M. (2020). Does time spent using social media impact mental health?: An eight year longitudinal study. *Computers in Human Behavior, 104*, 106–160. https://doi.org/10.1016/j.chb.2019.106160

Cyphers, B. (2019, September 18). Big tech's disingenuous push for a federal privacy law. Electronic Frontier Foundation. https://www.eff.org/deeplinks/2019/09/big-techs-disingenuous-push-federal-privacy-law

Darling, D. (2020, July 2). COVID-19 doesn't care about our political divide. In pandemic, we need to work together. https://www.usatoday.com/story/opinion/2020/07/02/covid-19-doesnt-care-americas-red-state-vs-blue-state-divide-column/5355387002

Dastin, J. (2018, October 10). Amazon scraps secret AI recruiting tool that showed bias against women. Reuters. https://www.reuters.com/article/us-amazon-com-jobs-automation-insight/amazon-scraps-secret-ai-recruiting-tool-that-showed-bias-against-women-idUSKCN1MK08G

Data and Statistics on children's mental health. (2020, June 15). https://www.cdc.gov/childrensmentalhealth/data.html

Davis, L. & Fry, R. (2019, July 31). College faculty have become more racially and ethnically diverse but remain far less so than students. Pew Research Center. https://www.pewresearch.org/fact-tank/2019/07/31/us-college-faculty-student-diversity

D'Cruz, P. & Noronha, E. (2016). Positives outweighing negatives: The experiences of Indian crowdsourced workers. *Work Organisation, Labour & Globalisation, 10*(1), 44–63. http://doi.org/10.13169/workorgalaboglob.10.1.0044

DiAngelo, R. J. (2018). *White fragility: Why it's so hard for white people to talk about racism.* Allen Lane, an imprint of Penguin Books.

Dobson, K., & Knezevic, I. (2017). 'Liking and sharing' the stigmatization of poverty and social welfare: Representations of poverty and welfare through Internet memes on social media. *tripleC: Communication, Capitalism & Critique. Journal for a Global Sustainable Information Society, 15*(2), 777–795. https://www.triple-c.at/index.php/tripleC/article/view/815

Doleac, J. L. (2017). The effects of DNA databases on crime. *American Economic Journal: Applied Economics, 9*(1), 165–201. https://doi.org/10.1257/app.20150043

Ekins, E. (2020, July 22). Poll: 62% of Americans say they have political view they are too afraid to share. Cato Institute. https://www.cato.org/publications/survey-reports/poll-62-americans-say-they-have-political-views-theyre-afraid-share?fbclid=IwAR2jW1qjZP3SQe04he5p6JVrjFQsn3m_9asm1mcJgSmT0y9zpsoo7ridhcM#introduction

Estlund, C. L. (2018, November). What should we do after work? Automation and employment law. *The Yale Law Journal, 128*(2), 254–543. https://www.yalelawjournal.org/pdf/Estlund_4opp7v2g.pdf

Federal Trade Commission. (2011, April 19). FTC seeks to halt 10 operators of fake news sites from making deceptive claims about acai berry weight loss products. https://www.ftc.gov/news-events/press-releases/2011/04/ftc-seeks-halt-10-operators-fake-news-sites-making-deceptive

Freelon, D., McIlwain, C. D., & Clark, M. (2016). Beyond the hashtags: #Ferguson, #Blacklivesmatter, and the online struggle for offline justice. Center for Media &

Social Impact, American University. https://cmsimpact.org/resource/beyond-hashtags -ferguson-blacklivesmatter-online-struggle-offline-justice

Fung, B. (2019, October 01). Appeals court upholds net neutrality rules but provides path for states to push back. CNN. https://www.cnn.com/2019/10/01/tech/net-neutrality -court-ruling/index.html

Goldblatt, H. (2020, July 31). A brief history of 'Karen.' *The New York Times*. https://www.nytimes.com/2020/07/31/style/karen-name-meme-history.html

Graham, M., & Shaw, J. (2017). *Towards a fairer gig economy*. Meatspace Press.

Gramlich, J. (2019, October 17). 5 facts about crime in the U.S. Pew Research Center. https://www.pewresearch.org/fact-tank/2019/10/17/facts-about-crime-in-the-u-s

Guadagno, R. E., Rempala, D. M., Murphy, S., & Okdie, B. M. (2013). What makes a video go viral? An analysis of emotional contagion and internet memes. *Computers in Human Behavior, 29*(6), 2312–2319. http://doi.org/10.1016/j.chb.2013.04.016

Harris, K., Kimson, A., & Schwedel, A. (2017, February 7). Labor 2030: The collision of demographics, automation and inequality. Bain & Company. https://www.bain.com/ insights/labor-2030-the-collision-of-demographics-automation-and-inequality

Haynes, T. (2018, May 01). Dopamine, smartphones & you: A battle for your time. Science in the News, Harvard Graduate School of the Arts and Sciences. http://sitn.hms.harvard .edu/flash/2018/dopamine-smartphones-battle-time

Heeks, R. (2017, August 2). Decent work and the digital gig economy: A developing country perspective on employment impacts and standards in online outsourcing, crowdwork, etc. *Development Informatics Working Paper, 71*. http://dx.doi.org/10.2139/ ssrn.3431033

Hern, A. (2020, April 07). WhatsApp to impose new limit on forwarding to fight fake news. *The Guardian*. https://www.theguardian.com/technology/2020/apr/07/whatsapp-to -impose-new-limit-on-forwarding-to-fight-fake-news

Hernandez, M., Raveendhran, R., Weingarten, E., & Barnett, M. (2019, August 21). How algorithms can diversify the startup pool. *MIT Sloan Management Review*. https:// sloanreview.mit.edu/article/how-algorithms-can-diversify-the-startup-pool

Hong, S., & Kim, S. H. (2016). Political polarization on Twitter: Implications for the use of social media in digital governments. *Government Information Quarterly, 33*(4), 777–782. https://doi.org/10.1016/j.giq.2016.04.007

Horowitz, J., & Graf, N. (2019, February 20). Most U.S. teens see anxiety, depression as major problems. Pew Research Center. https://www.pewsocialtrends.org/2019/02/20/ most-u-s-teens-see-anxiety-and-depression-as-a-major-problem-among-their-peers

Houser, K. (2020, July 12). Can AI solve the diversity problem in the tech industry? Mitigating noise and bias in employment decision-making. https://papers.ssrn.com/ sol3/papers.cfm?abstract_id=3344751

International Society for Technology in Education. (2016). *ISTE Standards for Students*. iste.org/standards/for-students

International Society for Technology in Education. (2017). *ISTE Standards for Educators*. iste.org/standards/for-educators

Iosifidis, P., & Nicoli, N. (2019). The battle to end fake news: A qualitative content analysis of Facebook announcements on how it combats disinformation. *International Communication Gazette, 82*(1), 60–81. https://doi.org/10.1177/1748048519880729

Israel, Elfie. (2002). Examining multiple perspectives in literature. In Holden, J., & Schmit, J. S. (Eds.). *Inquiry and the Literary Text: Constructing Discussions in the English Classroom. Classroom Practices in Teaching English, 32*. National Council of Teachers of English. https://files.eric.ed.gov/fulltext/ED471390.pdf

Jeong, S. (2019, April 10). Insurers want to know how many steps you took today. *The New York Times*. https://www.nytimes.com/2019/04/10/opinion/insurance-ai.html

Johnson, G. (2020, June 23). Police killings and Black mental health. Penn Today. https://penntoday.upenn.edu/news/police-killings-and-black-mental-health

Jones, A. (2019, January 30). First on CNN: NY Attorney General targets fake social media activity. CNN. https://www.cnn.com/2019/01/30/tech/new-york-attorney-general -social-media

Julian, S. B. (2020, April 27). What happened to American childhood? *The Atlantic*. https:// www.theatlantic.com/magazine/archive/2020/05/childhood-in-an-anxious-age/609079

Kaufman, S. (2020, July 19). 'It's not worth it': Young women on how TikTok has warped their body image. NBC News. https://www.nbcnews.com/tech/tech-news/it-s-not- worth-it-young-women-how-tiktok-has-n1234193

Kelly, Y., Zilanawala, A., Booker, C., & Sacker, A. (2018). Social media use and adolescent mental health: Findings from the UK Millennium Cohort Study. *EClinicalMedicine, 6*, 59–68. https://doi.org/10.1016/j.eclinm.2018.12.005

Kertysova, K. (2018). Artificial intelligence and disinformation: How AI changes the way disinformation is produced, disseminated, and can be countered. *Security & Human Rights, 29*(1–4), 55–81. https://doi.org/10.1163/18750230-02901005

Kim, M. (2016, November 11). How a researcher used big data to beat her own ovarian cancer. *The Washington Post*. https://www.washingtonpost.com/news/to-your-health/ wp/2016/11/11/how-a-researcher-used-her-computational-know-how-to-beat-her-own -ovarian-cancer

Klosowski, T. (2019, October 7). Your visitors deserve to know they're on camera. *The New York Times*. https://www.nytimes.com/2019/10/07/opinion/security-camera -privacy.html

Landi, H. (2020, July 15). UNC ties up with Google to launch mental health app for front- line workers. FierceHealthcare. https://www.fiercehealthcare.com/tech/unc-ties-up -google-to-launch-mental-health-app-for-frontline-workers

Leher, E. (2019, September 4). End the 'robots are coming for your job' panic. *Washington Examiner*. https://www.washingtonexaminer.com/opinion/end-the-robots-are-coming -for-your-job-panic

Levitsky, S., & Ziblatt, D. (2018). *How democracies die*. Broadway Books.

Lu, H., Li, Y., Chen, M., Kim, H., & Serikawa, S. (2017). Brain intelligence: Go beyond artificial intelligence. *Mobile Networks and Applications, 23*(2), 368–375. https://doi.org/ 10.1007/s11036-017-0932-8

Malik, F., Nicholson, B., & Heeks, R. (2017). Understanding the development implications of online outsourcing. In: Choudrie J., Islam M., Wahid F., Bass J., & Priyatma J. (Eds.). Information and communication technologies for development. ICT4D 2017. *IFIP Advances in Information and Communication Technology, 504*, 425–436. Springer. https://doi.org/10.1007/978-3-319-59111-7_35.

Manyika, J., Chui, M., Miremadi, M., Bughin, J., George, K., Willmott, P., & Dewhurst, M. (2017, January 12). Harnessing automation for a future that works. McKinsey Global Institute. https://www.mckinsey.com/featured-insights/digital-disruption/harnessing -automation-for-a-future-that-works#

Marantz, A. (2019, September 30). The dark side of techno-utopianism. *The New Yorker*. https://www.newyorker.com/magazine/2019/09/30/the-dark-side-of-techno-utopianism

Markkula Center for Applied Ethics at Santa Clara University. (n.d.). About the center. https://www.scu.edu/ethics/about-the-center

Mascarenhas, N. (2020, July 20). Dumpling launches to make anyone become their own Instacart. TechCrunch. https://techcrunch.com/2020/07/20/dumpling-launches-to -make-anyone-become-their-own-instacart

Matias, J. N. (2019). Preventing harassment and increasing group participation through social norms in 2,190 online science discussions. *Proceedings of the National Academy of Sciences, 116*(20), 9785–9789. https://doi.org/10.1073/pnas.1813486116

Mazambani, G., Carlson, M. A., Reysen, S., & Hempelmann, C. F. (2015). Impact of status and meme content on the spread of memes in virtual communities. *Human Technology: An Interdisciplinary Journal on Humans in ICT Environments, 11*(2), 148–164. https://doi.org/10.17011/ht/urn.201511113638

Mcdowell, Y. (2020). Smart security cameras: The corporatization of the surveillant assemblage. *The iJournal: Graduate Student Journal of the Faculty of Information, 5*(2). https://doi.org/10.33137/ijournal.v5i2.34416

McLaughlin, E. (2017, March 9). Peaches Monroe is taking back "on fleek" in the best way EVER. Teen Vogue. https://www.teenvogue.com/story/on-fleek-inventor-kayla -newman-aka-peaches-monroe-on-her-beauty-line

McLaughlin, E. C. (2017, April 26). Suspect OKs Amazon to hand over Echo recordings in murder case. CNN. https://www.cnn.com/2017/03/07/tech/amazon-echo-alexa -bentonville-arkansas-murder-case/index.html

McNeil C. (2017, April 2). Inside the metrics machine: USF uses big data to find, and help, overburdened students. *Tampa Bay Times*. https://www.tampabay.com/news/ education/college/inside-the-metrics-machine-usf-uses-big-data-to-find-and-help -overburdened/2318652

Mizzoni, J. (2017). *Ethics: The basics*. John Wiley & Sons.

Morrison, A. (2019). Laughing at injustice: #DistractinglySexy and #StayMadAbby as counternarratives. In Parry, D., Johnson, C., Fullagar, S. (Eds.). *Digital dilemmas: Transforming gender identities and power relations in everyday life*. Basingstoke, UK: Palgrave Macmillan. https://doi.org/10.1007/978-3-319-95300-7_2

Morse, A., & Wong, Q. (2020, June 4). K-pop stans take over racist hashtags on Twitter. CNET. https://www.cnet.com/news/k-pop-stans-take-over-racist-hashtags-on-twitter -bts

Mulligan, S. P., Linebaugh, C. D. (2019, March 25). Data Protection Law: An Overview (CRS Report No. R45631). Congressional Research Service. https://crsreports.congress .gov/product/pdf/R/R45631

Murrell, D. (2020, February 24). If you're a good citizen, delete the citizen policing app. *Philadelphia*. https://www.phillymag.com/news/2020/02/24/citizen-app-philadelphia

Naslund, J. A., Aschbrenner, K. A., Mchugo, G. J., Unützer, J., Marsch, L. A., & Bartels, S. J. (2017). Exploring opportunities to support mental health care using social media: A survey of social media users with mental illness. *Early Intervention in Psychiatry, 13*(3), 405–413. https://doi.org/10.1111/eip.12496

Noble, S. U. (2018). *Algorithms of oppression: How search engines reinforce racism*. New York University Press.

North, A. (2019, October 4). 7 positive changes that have come from the #MeToo movement. Vox. https://www.vox.com/identities/2019/10/4/20852639/me-too-movement -sexual-harassment-law-2019

Orben, A., & Przybylski, A. K. (2019). The association between adolescent well-being and digital technology use. *Nature Human Behaviour, 3*(2), 173–182. https://doi.org/10.1038/ s41562-018-0506-1

O'Sullivan, Andrea. (2019, February 5). Hate long TSA lines? Hate them enough to get your eye scanned instead? *Reason*. https://reason.com/2019/02/05/hate-long-tsa-lines-hate -them-enough-to

Pennycook, G., & Rand, D. G. (2019). Fighting misinformation on social media using crowdsourced judgments of news source quality. *Proceedings of the National Academy of Sciences, 116*(7), 2521–2526. https://doi.org/10.1073/pnas.1806781116

Piza, E. L., Welsh, B. C., Farrington, D. P., & Thomas, A. L. (2019). CCTV surveillance for crime prevention. *Criminology & Public Policy, 18*(1), 135–159. https://doi.org/10.1111/ 1745-9133.12419

Poli, R. (2017). Internet addiction update: Diagnostic criteria, assessment, and prevalence. *Neuropsychiatry, 07*(1), 4–8. https://doi.org/10.4172/Neuropsychiatry.1000171

Popper, N. (2020, January 17). Panicking about your kids' phones? New research says don't. *The New York Times*. https://www.nytimes.com/2020/01/17/technology/kids-smart phones-depression.html

PredPol. (2018, September 30). Predictive policing technology. https://www.predpol.com/ technology

Puzzanghera, J., & Guynn, J. (2010, April 7). Appeals court overturns FCC rule on net neutrality. *Los Angeles Times*. https://www.latimes.com/archives/la-xpm-2010-apr-07-la -fi-fcc-comcast7-2010apr07-story.html

Puzzanghera, J. (2015, February 27). FCC tightens internet oversight with new net neutrality rules. *Los Angeles Times*. https://www.latimes.com/business/la-fi-net-neutrality -vote-20150227-story.html

Puzzanghera, J. (2017, December 14). FCC votes to repeal net neutrality rules, a milestone for Republican deregulation push. *Los Angeles Times*. https://www.latimes.com/business/ la-fi-net-neutrality-fcc-20171214-story.html

Ranchordás, S. (2019). Nudging citizens through technology in smart cities. *International Review of Law, Computers & Technology, 34*(3) 254–276. https://doi.org/10.1080/13600 869.2019.1590928

Rayes, A. (2020, July 23). 'Pure Negativity': Division over pandemic creates challenges, opportunities in rural Facebook groups. KUNC. https://www.kunc.org/community/ 2020-07-23/pure-negativity-division-over-pandemic-creates-challenges-opportunities -in-rural-facebook-groups

Reardon, M. (2018, April 05). Your Alexa and Fitbit can testify against you in court. CNET. https://www.cnet.com/news/alexa-fitbit-apple-watch-pacemaker-can-testify-against-you-in-court

Rieland, R. (2018, March 5). Artificial intelligence is now used to predict crime. But is it biased? *Smithsonian Magazine*. https://www.smithsonianmag.com/innovation/artificial-intelligence-is-now-used-predict-crime-is-it-biased-180968337

Robb, A. (2017, November 16). Anatomy of a fake news scandal. *Rolling Stone*. https://www.rollingstone.com/politics/politics-news/anatomy-of-a-fake-news-scandal-125877

Robinson, P., Turk, D., Jilka, S., & Cella, M. (2018). Measuring attitudes towards mental health using social media: Investigating stigma and trivialisation. *Social Psychiatry and Psychiatric Epidemiology, 54*(1), 51–58. https://doi.org/10.1007/s00127-018-1571-5

Rolston, M. (2019, October 25). The tecno-utopian visions of Google and Facebook are dead. What comes next? *Fast Company*. www.fastcompany.com/90422013/techno-utopianism-is-dead-what-comes-next

Rosenblat, A. (2018, October 12). When your boss is an algorithm. *The New York Times*. https://www.nytimes.com/2018/10/12/opinion/sunday/uber-driver-life.html

Rosenblat, A. (2020, July 3). Gig workers are here to stay. It's time to give them benefits. *Harvard Business Review*. https://hbr.org/2020/07/gig-workers-are-here-to-stay-its-time-to-give-them-benefits

Samuel, S. (2020, March 12). These apps make a game out of relieving anxiety. They may be onto something. Vox. https://www.vox.com/the-highlight/2019/9/17/20863016/anxiety-app-phone-gamification

Savage, C. (2019, July 9). Trump can't block critics from his Twitter account, appeals court rules. *The New York Times*. https://www.nytimes.com/2019/07/09/us/politics/trump-twitter-first-amendment.html

Schatz, A., & Raice, S. (2010, December 22). Internet gets new rules of the road. *The Wall Street Journal*. https://www.wsj.com/articles/SB10001424052748703581204576033513990668654

Schuppe, J. (2019, May 11). How facial recognition became a routine policing tool in America. NBC News. https://www.nbcnews.com/news/us-news/how-facial-recognition-became-routine-policing-tool-america-n1004251

Selk, A. (2018, April 28). The ingenious and 'dystopian' DNA technique police used to hunt the 'Golden State Killer' suspect. *The Salt Lake Tribune*. https://www.sltrib.com/news/nation-world/2018/04/28/the-ingenious-and-dystopian-dna-technique-police-used-to-hunt-the-golden-state-killer-suspect

Simonite, T. (2020, May 12). Facebook's AI for hate speech improves. How much is unclear. *Wired*. https://www.wired.com/story/facebook-ai-hate-speech-improves-unclear

Singer, N., & Sang-Hun, C. (2020, March 23). As coronavirus surveillance escalates, personal privacy plummets. *The New York Times*. https://www.nytimes.com/2020/03/23/technology/coronavirus-surveillance-tracking-privacy.html

Smith, C. S. (2020, April 8). Want to be better at sports? Listen to the machines. *The New York Times*. https://www.nytimes.com/2020/04/08/technology/ai-sports-athletes-machine-learning.html

Spangler, T. (2020, June 30). Reddit finally bans hate speech, removes 2,000 racist and violent forums including The_Donald. *Variety*. https://variety.com/2020/digital/news/reddit-bans-hate-speech-groups-removes-2000-subreddits-donald-trump-1234692898

Spectre, R. (2017) Erase Donald Trump from the internet. Trump Filter. http://trumpfilter.com

Staff, P. (2020). Net neutrality timeline. ProQuest. https://explore.proquest.com/sirsissuesresearcher/document/2250548492?accountid=80527

Stephens-Davidowitz, S. (2017). *Everybody lies: Big data, new data, and what the Internet can tell us about who we really are*. HarperCollins.

Sydell, L. (2016, November 23). We tracked down a fake-news creator in the suburbs. Here's what we learned. NPR. https://www.npr.org/sections/alltechconsidered/2016/11/23/503146770/npr-finds-the-head-of-a-covert-fake-news-operation-in-the-suburbs

Taneja, H. (2019, January 23). The era of "move fast and break things" is over. *Harvard Business Review*. https://hbr.org/2019/01/the-era-of-move-fast-and-break-things-is-over

The New York Times. (2018, April 10). Mark Zuckerberg testimony: Senators question Facebook's commitment to privacy. https://www.nytimes.com/2018/04/10/us/politics/mark-zuckerberg-testimony.html

Thompson, S. A., & Warzel, C. (2019, December 19). Twelve million phones, one dataset, zero privacy. *The New York Times*. https://www.nytimes.com/interactive/2019/12/19/opinion/location-tracking-cell-phone.html

Thorstad, R., Wolff, P. (2019). Predicting future mental illness from social media: A big-data approach. *Behav Res Methods*, 51(4), 1586–1600. https://doi.org/10.3758/s13428-019-01235-z

Tippens, W. (2017). Memes follow free market principles. *Gale Opposing Viewpoints Online Collection*. Gale. https://link.gale.com/apps/doc/UXKFOS475996065/OVIC?u=nape28931&sid=OVIC&xid=b56cf873

Trump, D. J. [@realdonaldtrump]. (2020, October 16). *Twitter Shuts Down Entire Network To Slow Spread Of Negative Biden News https://Babylonbee.com/news/twitter-shuts-down-entire-network-to-slow-spread-of-negative-biden-news via @TheBabylonBee Wow, this has never been* [Tweet]. Twitter. https://twitter.com/realDonaldTrump/status/1317044556328730625

Tucker, J. A. (2017, April 11). Hey "New York Times": This is why Uber is awesome. Medium. https://medium.com/fee-org/hey-new-york-times-this-is-why-uber-is-awesome-jeffrey-a-tucker-cde38aab04e4

U.S. Department of Health and Human Services, National Institute of Mental Health. (2017). Any anxiety disorder. https://www.nimh.nih.gov/health/statistics/any-anxiety-disorder.shtml

U.S. Department of Justice. (2020a, January). 32. Video surveillance—use of closed circuit television (CCTV). https://www.justice.gov/archives/jm/criminal-resource-manual-32-video-surveillance-use-closed-circuit-television-cctv

U.S. Department of Justice (2020b, January). 9-7.200. Video surveillance—closed circuit television—Department of Justice approval required when there is a reasonable expectation of privacy. https://www.justice.gov/jm/jm-9-7000-electronic-surveillance#9-7.200

Video Voyeurism Prevention Act of 2004, Pub. L. No 108-495, codified at 18 U.S.C. §1801.

Vittert, L. (2020, June 11). Are conspiracy theories on the rise in the US? The Conversation. https://theconversation.com/are-conspiracy-theories-on-the-rise-in-the-us-121968

Wachter-Boettcher, S. (2017). *Technically wrong: sexist apps, biased algorithms, and other threats of toxic tech*. W.W. Norton & Company.

Waldman, A. (2018). The marketplace of fake news. *University of Pennsylvania Journal of Constitutional Law, 20*(4), 845–870. https://scholarship.law.upenn.edu/jcl/vol20/iss4/3

Walt Disney World. (n.d.). My Disney experience—frequently asked questions. https://disneyworld.disney.go.com/faq/my-disney-experience/my-magic-plus-privacy

West, S. M., Whittaker, M., & Crawford, K. (2019). *Discriminating systems: Gender, race, and power in AI*. AI Now Institute. https://ainowinstitute.org/discriminatingsystems.html

Wihbey, J., Joseph, K., & Lazer, D. (2018). The social silos of journalism? Twitter, news media and partisan segregation. *New Media & Society, 21*(4), 815–835. https://doi.org/10.1177/1461444818807133

Wortham, J. (2011, April 09). Feel like a wallflower? Maybe it's your Facebook wall. *The New York Times*. https://www.nytimes.com/2011/04/10/business/10ping.html?src=recg

Yurieff, K. (2019a, September 3). YouTube says it's removing more hate speech than before but controversial channels remain up. CNN. https://www.cnn.com/2019/09/03/tech/youtube-hate-speech/index.html

Yurieff, K. (2019b, November 14). Instagram is now testing hiding likes worldwide. CNN. www.cnn.com/2019/11/14/tech/instagram-hiding-likes-globally/index.html

Yurieff, K. (2020, June 29). YouTube removes Richard Spencer and David Duke a year after saying it would ban supremacists. CNN. https://www.cnn.com/2020/06/29/tech/white-supremacists-youtube/index.html

Zito, S. (2020). Social media does not reflect the real America. In *Gale Opposing Viewpoints Online Collection*. Gale. (Reprinted from The perils of trading social interaction for social media, *Washington Examiner*, 2019, August 18.) https://link.gale.com/apps/doc/EGEVZE488199519/OVIC?u=uiuc_uc&sid=OVIC&xid=03116e1d

Index

NUMBERS

4chan and 8chan, 24, 125
8kun, 125
60 seconds online, events during, 43

A

A/B testing, 43–44
Abedjan et al., 50
addictions related to internet, 104–105
adolescent health and well-being, 114
Affectiva software, 98
affinity-mapping activity, 118–119
Alexa court cases, Googling, 41
algorithm
    boss as, 91–92
    defined, 67
algorithmic bias, defined, 67
Algorithms of Oppression, 76, 145
Alia and Thumbtack platforms, 94–95
Amazon, artificial intelligence (AI) recruiting tool,
    77
amendments to U.S. Constitution, 46
America, reflection on social media, 130–133
American childhood, considering, 115
The American Meme, 145
American Psychiatric Association, 104
anchoring bias, 23
Anderson, J., & Rainie, L., 32
Andersson, H., 107
Andorfer, A., 28–30
anxiety and depression, rise of, 103–104
"anxiety consumerism," 110–111
anxiety disorders, defined, 103
Anzilotti, E., 94
app design, psychology of, 107
Aquinas, Thomas, 7
arguments
    artificial intelligence (AI), 72–78

big data, 49–54
biometrics, 54–56
breaking down, 26–28
considering, 14–15
disinformation online, 28–30
mental health concerns, 108–115
regulation, 31–33
surveillance, 54–60
tech companies and misinformation, 33–35
technological innovation and jobs, 89–95
Aristotle, 6
Arthur, R., 24
artificial intelligence (AI)
    arguments, 72–78
    in decision-making, 68–72
    defined, 66–67
    ethical concerns, 80–81
    in hiring, 69–70
    and job displacement, 90
    in law enforcement, 70–72
    and machine learning, 90
    uses and limitations of, 67–68
Artificial Unintelligence, 69
audio resources, 145
Automating Inequality, 145
automation, concerns about, 85–86, 90
Automation in the Workplace, 86

B

Baby Boomers, retirement of, 89
Barnard, M., 126
Behind the Screen, 145
Benjamin, Ruha, 79
Bentham, Jeremy, 7
bias
    effects of, 24
    types of, 23
Biden, Joe, 22, 143–144

big data
    arguments, 49–54
    discussing, 62–64
    uses of, 43–45
biometrics
    defined, 44
    and surveillance, 54–56
    uses of, 45–46
"black girls," Google search for, 76
Black mental health and police killings, 113
Black Mirror, 125, 145
#BlackLivesMatter
    hashtag, 134
    protests, 32–33
Boburg, S., & Bennett, D., 132
book resources, 145
Bored and Brilliant, 116, 145
bosses as algorithms, 91–92
"Boston's Safest Driver" app, 52
Bousquet, C., 53
boyd, danah, 121–122
Bradbury, Ray, 125
Brennan, Fredrick, 125
Brigham Young University research, 113–114
Brooks, Rayshard, 113
Broussard, Meredith, 69
"bubble," getting trapped in, 23

C
California Consumer Privacy Act, 48
CARES Act, 92
carousel discussion protocol, 37–40
Carter, Deborah, 61
CASEL (Collaborative for Academic, Social, and Emotional Learning), 10–11
Castile, Philando, 113
CBC Radio, 41
CCTV (closed-circuit television), 55
CDC (Centers for Disease Control and Prevention), 103–104
Ceccato, V., 57
censoring content, 20
Center for Media and Social Impact, 134
CFAA (Computer Fraud and Abuse Act), 47
Chang, Karen, 140
Chang, Robin, 116–118
Chappell, B., 139
Chicago Tribune, 133
childhood in America, considering, 115

Chowdhury & Sadek, 68
Chrome, Trump Filter for, 26–27
Ciccone, Michelle, 79–80
Citizen Educator Standard, 40, 63, 99
Citizen Policing App, 58–59
civil liberties, arguments, 51–54
Clear, appearance in airports, 45
Coler, Jestin, 28–30
Collins, B., 32
Collins, K., & Dance, G. J., 54
commercial regulation, 28–30
community-based regulation, 31–33
compulsive behaviors, 105
computer addiction, 105
concentric circle discussion strategy, 62–64
Confederate flags, 132
confirmation bias, 23
Consequentialism, 61
conspiracy theories
    abundance of, 133
    defined, 123
constitutional amendments, 46
consumers and producers, tech ethics for, 9–10
content moderation, 33–34, 37–40. *See also* social media
Convertino, J., 35
COPPA laws, 47
COVID-19 pandemic
    combating misinformation on, 35
    division over, 128–129
    impact on first responders, 110
    impact on healthcare workers, 110
    surveillance and personal privacy, 53–54
    and unemployment insurance, 92
    working together during, 129–130
Cowgill, Bo, 73
Coyne et al., 114
crime, reduction of, 54–56
crowdsourcing, 31
cyberbullying, applying ethical frameworks to, 7–9
cyber-relational addiction, 105
cybersexual addiction, 105
Cyphers, B., 48

D
Darling, D., 129
Dastin, J., 77
data, pervasiveness of, 42–46
data doppelgangers, seeking out, 43–44

data privacy
    defined, 44
    laws around, 47
data profiles, creation of, 44
Davis, L., & Fry, R., 76
D'Cruz, P., & Noronha, E., 93
DeAngelo, Joseph James, 56
decision-making responsibility, CASEL Core SEL Competency, 11
decisions, making and testing, 15
democracy, threats to, 25–26
"Denver Guardian," 28–30
Deontological Ethics, 7, 9
depression and anxiety, rise of, 103–104
Designer Educator Standard, 81, 99, 119
Devumi case, settlement of, 30
DiAngelo, R. J., 68
DigCitCommit initiative, 2
Digital Citizen Student Standard, 40, 63, 119
digital citizenship, expanding definition of, 1, 121
Digital Citizenship in Action, 1
digital ethics
    for consumers and producers, 9–10
    explained, 6, 8
    and ISTE Standards for Students, 11–12
    and SEL (social and emotional learning), 10
"Discriminating Systems: Gender, Race, and Power in AI," 76
discussions
    carousel protocol, 37–40
    concentric circle strategy, 62–64
    pyramid type, 141–142
    tips for, 12–18
Disinfomedia, 28–30
disinformation. *See also* information warfare; misinformation
    conundrum of, 21–24
    defined, 21
    regulation online, 28–30
Disney parks, data collected by, 48–49
#Distractinglysexy Tweets, 139
DNA profiles, use of, 55–56
Dobson, K., & Knezevic, I., 138
Doleac, J. L., 55
"downblousing" and "upskirting," 48
DSM-5 (*Diagnostic and Statistical Manual of Mental Disorders*), 104
Duke, David, 25
Dumpling shopping app, 94–95

dystopia and utopia, relating to technology, 124–125

E
echo chambers, defined, 21, 23–24
Edinburgh, increasing recycling in, 52–53
Eighth Grade, 145
electronic surveillance. *See* surveillance technologies
Eliza chatbot, 96–97
Empowered Learner Student Standard, 63, 141
environment, considering in discussions, 17
Estlund, C. L., 90
ethical frameworks, defined, 8
ethical issues, recognizing, 13–14
ethical theories, 6–7
ethical thinking, teaching process of, 13–15
ethicists, theories used by, 61
ethics, defined, 8
ethnic slurs, increase in, 24
Eubanks, Virginia, 145
Everybody Lies, 42

F
Facebook
    artificial intelligence for hate speech, 75
    detecting disinformation, 34
    "liking" friends on, 23
    myPersonality app, 54
    in rural areas, 128–129
    and "wiring the world," 124
facial recognition, 56
Facilitator Educator Standard, 40, 81, 99, 119, 141
fact-checking, 33–34
facts, getting, 14
Fake, Caterina, 97, 145
fake news
    defined, 21
    fighting, 31
    rise in rhetoric around, 2
    terminology, 22
fake social media activity, targeting, 30. *See also* social media
FCRA laws, 47
Fifth Amendment, 46
filter bubble, defined, 21, 23
First Amendment, 46
first responders and anxiety, 110
flag-burning hoax, 132
Floyd, George, 32–33, 113, 135, 143

FOMO (fear of missing out), 106
Fourth Amendment, 46
Fox News, 23
free speech, regulating, 29
freelancers/independent contractors, defined, 86–87
Freelon et al., 135
FTC (Federal Trade Commission), 29–30

G
Garner, Eric, 113
gig economy
    beneficial aspects of, 93–94
    explained, 86–87
    joining, 84
    providing benefits to workers, 92
GLBA laws, 47
Goldblatt, H., 139
Goldblum, Jeff, 101
"Golden State Killer," 56
Goldman, Alex and PJ Vogt, 145
Google Chrome extensions, 26
Google Duplex virtual assistant, 98
Google searches
    "beautiful," 76
    "black girls," 76
    "professor style," 76
Graham & Shaw, 94
Gramlich, J., 55
Green, Stefanie, 35–37
Guadagno et al., 138

H
Halo Neuroscience headset, 98
Harris, Kamala, 143–144
Harris et al., 90
"Harrison Bergeron," 65, 68
hashtag, defined, 123
hashtag activism
    perspectives about, 133–136
    vocabulary, 123
hate, platforms for, 24–25, 75
hate speech, defined, 21
Haynes, T., 107
health and wellness, considering in discussions, 16–17
health conditions, discussion online, 112
healthcare workers and anxiety, 110
Heeks, R., 93
helicopter parenting, 115

Hern, A., 35
Hernandez et al., 74
Herndon & Searcey, 135
Heroes Help app, 110
HIPAA laws, 47
hiring, artificial intelligence (AI) in, 69–70
hoaxes in social media, 132
Hobbes, Thomas, 7
Hogan, Amanda, 96–97
home-security systems, popularity of, 58
Hong & Kim, 128
Horowitz, J., & Graf, N., 104
Houser, Kimberly A., 73
Hughes, Chris, 124
human bias, defined, 67
humans, outperformance of technology, 90
Hunt, Tim, 139
HyperDocs, using, 36–37

I
Illinois Biometric Information Privacy Act, 48
independent contractors/freelancers, 86–87
information overload, 105
information warfare, threat of, 2. *See also* disinformation; misinformation
Innovative Designer Student Standard, 40, 81, 99, 119
Instagram, 118
insurance companies, 77–78
internet
    perspectives about, 122–123
    and social media, 126
internet addiction
    explained, 103–105
    FOMO and internet anxieties, 106
internet anxieties and FOMO, 106
internet awareness exercises, 116–118
internet rules vs. community-based regulation, 31–33
Iosifidis, P., & Nocoli, N., 34
Irvin Painter, Nell, 135
Israel, Elfie, 12
ISTE Standards for Educators
    3b: Citizen, 40, 99
    3d: Citizen, 63
    5b: Designer, 81, 99, 119
    6a: Facilitator, 99, 119, 141
    6c: Facilitator, 81
    6d: Facilitator, 40, 141

ISTE Standards for Students
  1d: Empowered Learner, 63, 141
  2a: Digital Citizen, 40
  2b: Digital Citizen, 119
  2d: Digital Citizen, 63
  3d: Knowledge Constructor, 40, 63, 81, 99,
    119, 141
  4d: Innovative Designer, 40, 81, 99, 119
  and tech ethics, 11–12
It's Complicated: The Social Lives of Networked Teens,
  121

J

Jaffee, Sara, 113
James, Letitia, 30
Jeong, S., 77
job automation, 85–86. *See also* labor; online labor;
  technological innovation and jobs; work
John Hancock insurance company, 77
Johnson, G., 113
Jones, A., 30
journalism, 128
Julian, S. B., 115
Jurassic Park, 101

K

Kant, Immanuel, 7
Kantianism, 61
"Karen," 139–140
Kaufman, S., 112
Kelly et al., 112
Kenney, Kate, 129
Kertysova, K., 34
Kim, M., 50
Klosowski, T., 59
knowledge and vocation, considering in
  discussions, 16
Knowledge Constructor Student Standard, 40, 63,
  81, 99, 119, 141
K-pop artists, response to hate speech, 33

L

labor, predicted scarcity of, 90. *See also* job
  automation; online labor; technological
  innovation and jobs; work
Landi, H., 110
law enforcement, artificial intelligence (AI) in,
  70–72. *See also* Mapping Police Violence; police
  killings and Black mental health

laws
  data privacy, 47
  surveillance and personal privacy, 47–48
learning, presenting, 100
Lehrer, E., 86
Levitsky, Steven, 25
library collections, 126
literature, role of humanity and morality in, 5
location tracking services, using, 45–46, 59–60
Long, Kayla, 112
Lord of the Flies, 5
Lu et al., 68

M

machine learning and artificial intelligence, 90
MagicBands, data collected by, 48–49
Malcolm, Ian, 101–102
Malik et al., 93
Manyika et al., 91
Mapping Police Violence, 135. *See also* police
  killings and Black mental health
Marantz, A., 124
Markkula Center for Applied Ethics at Santa Clara
  University, 13
Martin, Trayvon, 134
Mascarenhas, N., 94
Mazambani et al., 138
McDowell, Y., 58
McKinsey Global Institute research, 90
McLaughlin, E., 41
McLean, Sam, 110
McNeil, C., 51
meme
  culture and values, 136–139
  defined, 123
mental health concerns
  affinity-mapping activity, 118–119
  anxiety and depression, 103–104
  FOMO and internet anxieties, 106
  increase in, 102–103
  internet addiction, 104–105
  psychology of app design, 107
  and technology, 108–115
mental health disorder, defined, 103
#MeToo movement, 136
Minneapolis Police Department, 135, 143
minority communities, threats of violence against, 24
misinformation. *See also* disinformation;
  information warfare

conundrum of, 21–24
defined, 21
"Miss Ann," 139–140
Mizzoni, J., 7
Modulate voice skins, 98
moral lens, applying to discussions, 16
morals, defined, 8
Morse, A., & Wong, Q., 32–33
Mosseri, Adam, 118
Mulligan, S. P., & Linebaugh, C. D., 47
Murrell, D., 58
myPersonality app, 54

N

"nanny cams," use of, 59
Naslund et al., 110
Natural Law Ethics, 7–8
negativity over pandemic, 128–129
Nest home-security systems, popularity of, 58
New Orleans, texting campaign in, 53
The New York Times, 133, 145
The New Yorker, 125
NewTechKids education academy, 60–62
Nextdoor app, 58
Noble, Safiya Umoja, 76, 145
Note to Self, 145
novels, role of humanity and morality in, 5
nudging with big data, 52–53

O

O'Neal, Cathy, 145
The Onion, 21
online labor, beneficial aspects of, 93–94. *See also* job automation; labor; technological innovation and jobs; work
optimism
and pessimism, 126
and pragmatism, 125–126
options, exploring, 14–15
Orben, A., and Przybylski, A. K., 114
O'Sullivan, Andrea, 45
outcomes, reflecting on, 15

P

partisan polarization, defined, 123
peer-to-peer marketplace, defined, 86
Pennycook and Rand, research of, 31
Pepke, Shirley, 50–51
personal digital ethics, defined, 8

personal privacy
arguments, 51–54
and COVID-19 surveillance, 53–54
laws around, 47–48
personalization, pros and cons of, 23
pessimism and optimism, 126
Pew Research Center, 32
Philadelphia, use of Citizen crime-reporting app in, 58–59
phones, time spent on, 115
Piza et al., 55
#Pizzagate, 19–20
Poli, R., 105
police killings and Black mental health, 113. *See also* law enforcement; Mapping Police Violence
political and social division, 127–130
"Politically Incorrect" 4chan board, 24
Popper, N., 115
PredPol database, 71
privacy
discussing, 62–64
right to, 46–48
producers and consumers, tech ethics for, 9–10
pyramid discussions, 141–142

Q

QR codes
artificial intelligence (AI), 81
audio resources, 145
book resources, 145
ISTE Standards for Educators, 12
ISTE Standards for Students, 12
mental health and technology, 120
privacy, 64
regulation of internet, 40
social media, 141–142
technological innovation and jobs, 100
video resources, 145

R

Rabbit Hole, 145
Race After Technology, 79
racial slurs, increase in, 24
Rahuba, Adam, 132–133
Ranchordás, S., 52, 53
Reardon, M., 41
Reddit, policies of, 24
regulating, disinformation online, 28–30
regulation

at community level, 31–33
    of free speech, 29
relationship skills, CASEL Core SEL Competency, 11
religious slurs, increase in, 24
Reply All, 145
responsible decision-making, CASEL Core SEL Competency, 11
Richmond, Jennifer, 35–37
Rittenhouse, Kyle, 143
Robb, A., 20
Roberts, Sarah T., 145
Robinson, Turk, Jilka, and Cella, 112
robots and job displacement, 90
Rolston, M., 126
Rosenblat, A., 91–92
Russian interference in 2016 U.S. presidential election, 2

S
Samuel, S., 110
satire, mistaking for fact, 22
Schuppe, J., 56
Scott, Walter, 113
security technologies, opinions about, 59–60
SEL (social and emotional learning), 10–11
self-awareness, CASEL Core SEL Competency, 11
self-censorship
    defined, 123
    rise of, 130–131
self-management, CASEL Core SEL Competency, 11
self-service machines, use of, 85
Selk, A., 56
sexual harassment, 136
sharing economy, explained, 86, 88
SHEG (Stanford History Education Group), 36–37
Should This Exist? exercise, engaging in, 97–100, 145
Silicon Valley, 102, 124
Simonite, T., 75
Singer, N., & Sang-Hun, C., 53
Sinyangwe, Samuel, 135
"smart cities," use of big data in, 52–53
Smart Insights, 43
smartphones, time spent on, 115
Smith, C. S., 74
social and political division, 127–130
social awareness, CASEL Core SEL Competency, 11

Social Contract Ethics, 7–8
The Social Dilemma, 140–141, 145
social lens, applying to discussions, 16
social media. *See also* content moderation; fake social media activity
    hashtag activism, 133–136
    hoaxes, 132
    and internet, 126
    and mental health concerns, 110, 111–113
    political and social division, 127
    reflection of America, 130–133
    and society, 122
society, collective conscious of, 101–102
Socratic seminars, holding, 12–13
Spangler, T., 24
Spectre, R., 26
sports, using artificial intelligence (AI) in, 74–75
Spotts Cobbley, Kristie, 128–129
statistics
    anxiety and depression, 103–104
    displacement of workers, 90
    human outperformance of technology, 90–91
    mental health concerns, 109
    platforms for hate, 24
    police violence against African Americans, 135
    removal of misinformation, 33–34
    self-censorship, 130–131
    unemployment insurance, 92
Stephens-Davidowitz, S., 42–43, 50
Stockholm, study of surveillance in, 57
student records, metrics related to, 51
student thinking, challenging, 99
surveillance technologies
    arguments, 56–60
    and biometric records, 54–56
    defined, 44
    laws around, 47–48
    uses of, 45–46
Sydell, L., 28–30

T
Taneja, H., 124
Taylor, Breonna, 135
tech companies and misinformation, 33–35
tech ethics
    for consumers and producers, 9–10
    explained, 6, 8
    and ISTE Standards for Students, 11–12
    and SEL (social and emotional learning), 10

Technically Wrong, 76–77
technochauvinism, 69
technological dystopia, 125
technological innovation and jobs, 89–95. *See also* job automation; labor; online labor; work
technological utopia, 124
technology
        impact on users, 96–97
        key questions related to, 6
        unintended consequences of, 102
techno-optimism and techno-pragmatism, 125–126
teens, awareness of mental health concerns, 104
Terms and Conditions May Apply, 145
Third Amendment, 46
Thompson, S. A., & Warzel, C., 46
Thorstad, R., & Wolff, P., 109
Thumbtack and Alia platforms, 94–95
TikTok
        and body image of women, 112
        collaboration with WHO (World Health Organization), 35
Time's Up Legal Defense Fund, 136
Tippens, W., 137
To Kill a Mockingbird, 5
Todd, Brad, 131–132
Trump, Donald, 22, 26–27, 135, 144
Trump Filter Chrome extension, 26–27
Tucker, J. A., 87
Turner, Matthew, 80–81
Twitter, 127–128
        fighting misinformation, 32

U
Uber drivers
        and algorithmic "boss," 91–92
        tax implications, 92
UNC Health, 110
unemployment insurance, applications for, 92
"upskirting" and "downblousing," 48
U.S. Department of Health and Human Services, 104
U.S. Department of Justice, 47
U.S. government, regulation of disinformation online, 28–30
USF (University of South Florida), 51
Utilitarian Ethics, 7–8
utopia and dystopia, relating to technology, 124–125

V
The Verge, 145
video resources, 145
Video Voyeurism Prevention Act of 2004, 47–48
violence, threats of, 24
viral content, 137–138
Virtue Ethics, 6–7, 61
Vittert, L., 133
vocabulary
        algorithm, 67
        algorithmic bias, 67
        anxiety disorders, 103
        artificial intelligence (AI), 67
        big data, 44
        biometrics, 44
        conspiracy theory, 123
        data privacy, 44
        digital ethics/tech ethics, 8
        disinformation, 21
        echo chambers, 21
        ethical frameworks, 8
        ethics, 8
        fake news, 21
        filter bubble, 21
        gig economy, 86
        hashtag, 123
        hashtag activism, 123
        hate speech, 21
        human bias, 67
        independent contractors/freelancers, 86
        internet addiction, 103
        meme, 123
        mental health disorder, 103
        misinformation, 21
        morals, 8
        partisan polarization, 123
        peer-to-peer marketplace, 86
        personal digital ethics, 8
        self-censorship, 123
        sharing economy, 86
        surveillance technologies, 44
        tech ethics/digital ethics, 8
Vogt, PJ and Alex Goldman, 145
Vonnegut, Kurt, 65

W
Wachter-Boettcher, Sara, 76–77
Waldman, A., 24, 30
Walt Disney World, 48–49

Washington Examiner, 131
Washington Post, 132
Weapons of Math, 145
Welch, Edgar Maddison, 19–20
wellness and health, considering in discussions, 16–17
West et al., 76
#WhatIAteInaDay, 112
WhatsApp, response to fake news, 35
#WhiteOutWednesday, 33
Whitmer, Gretchen, 143
WHO (World Health Organization), collaboration with TikTok, 35
Why'd You Push That Button, 145
Wihbey, J., Joseph, K., and Lazer, D., 128
Woebot virtual therapist, 98
women
     and #MeToo movement, 136

in science labs, 139
work, future of, 84. *See also* job automation; labor; technological innovation and jobs
workers, displacement of, 90. *See also* job automation; technological innovation and jobs
Wortham, J., 106

Y

Yeh, Tom, 80
YouTube, hate-speech policy, 25
Yurieff, K., 25, 118

Z

Ziblatt, Daniel, 25
Zito, Salena, 131–132
Zomorodi, Manoush, 116, 145
Zuckerberg, Mark, 25–26, 124

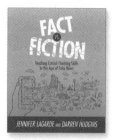